Praise for *The Internet to the Inner-Net*

'Drawing from his cultural foundations in Eastern wisdom originating in India, training in yoga and meditation, and solid experience in and understanding of the world of digital technology and Silicon Valley, Gopi has skillfully created a practical user manual for navigating through it all. Most important, he shows us how to live a full life of joy, intent and purpose.'

— **Chade-Meng Tan**, Jolly Good Fellow of Google and bestselling author of *Search Inside Yourself*

'Gopi is one of a kind, an incredibly busy executive who knows and lives from a deep inner place. He shows in this exquisite book a path that marries the world of Doing (Actions, Results, Deadlines) and that of Being (Presence, Spaciousness, Connection). For those who want to be actively engaged in the world of business and commerce, and stay present and attuned while doing so, this book is for you. I cannot think of a better guide for this.'

— **Soren Gordhamer**, founder, Wisdom 2.0 movement

'Gopi Kallayil's compelling new book is a reminder that service to humanity – not glorification of the self – is the greatest calling for any human. Most of us do not have the opportunities that Gopi's amazing career at Google has made available to him. But all of us have the opportunity to live humbly, observe the world around us and help others whenever we can. That is the message of Gopi's book, and it is a message that deserves our closest attention.'

— **G. Richard Shell**, Thomas Gerrity Professor, The Wharton School of Business, and author of *Springboard: Launching Your Personal Search for Success*

'You may not think of Silicon Valley as synonymous with mindful living and soulful, reflective inner work – but Gopi Kallayil bridges the gap brilliantly, both in his own life and in this guide to optimizing your personal network of mind, body and spirit.'

— **Congressman Tim Ryan**, author of *A Mindful Nation* and *The Real Food Revolution*

The
Internet
to the
Inner-Net

The
Internet
to the
Inner-Net

Five Ways to Reset Your Connection
and Live a Conscious Life

GOPI KALLAYIL

HAY HOUSE

Carlsbad, California • New York City • London • Sydney
Johannesburg • Vancouver • Hong Kong • New Delhi

First published and distributed in the United Kingdom by:
Hay House UK Ltd, Astley House, 33 Notting Hill Gate, London W11 3JQ
Tel: +44 (0)20 3675 2450; Fax: +44 (0)20 3675 2451; www.hayhouse.co.uk

Published and distributed in the United States of America by:
Hay House Inc., PO Box 5100, Carlsbad, CA 92018-5100
Tel: (1) 760 431 7695 or (800) 654 5126
Fax: (1) 760 431 6948 or (800) 650 5115; www.hayhouse.com

Published and distributed in Australia by:
Hay House Australia Ltd, 18/36 Ralph St, Alexandria NSW 2015
Tel: (61) 2 9669 4299; Fax: (61) 2 9669 4144; www.hayhouse.com.au

Published and distributed in the Republic of South Africa by:
Hay House SA (Pty) Ltd, PO Box 990, Witkoppen 2068
info@hayhouse.co.za; www.hayhouse.co.za

Published and distributed in India by:
Hay House Publishers India, Muskaan Complex, Plot No.3, B-2,
Vasant Kunj, New Delhi 110 070
Tel: (91) 11 4176 1620; Fax: (91) 11 4176 1630; www.hayhouse.co.in

Distributed in Canada by:
Raincoast Books, 2440 Viking Way, Richmond, B.C. V6V 1N2
Tel: (1) 604 448 7100; Fax: (1) 604 270 7161; www.raincoast.com

A catalogue record for this book is available from the British Library.

ISBN: 978-1-78180-256-4

Cover design: Leanne Siu Anastasi; Interior design: Nick C. Welch

Printed and bound by CPI Group (UK) Ltd, Croydon, CR0 4YY

Dedicated to my parents
and to my spiritual teachers
Rama Devi, Tara Devi, and Amma

CONTENTS

FOREWORD

recharge

I thought I knew Gopi Kallayil a little, until he handed me a CD he'd just recorded of himself singing lead vocals on a set of call-and-response songs in the Bhakti yoga tradition. This came at the end of a bright winter day in which he'd been showing me around his mind-boggling facilities at the Google headquarters in Mountain View, California, pointing out the rolling green hills on which he takes meetings and leading me across the open space on which he's been training yoga students and teachers from within his company for years. It came after he'd told me about his adventures giving talks around the world— on marketing and mindfulness in the same unexpected breath—and filled in a little of the story you're about to read, of how he arrived in a forgotten Californian suburb full of Afghan taxi drivers and half-fugitive South Asians, not having enough money to attend the colleges that had accepted him, used most of his scanty savings to rent a flat, buy an old Honda, and join Toastmasters International, and somehow, against all odds, laid claim to the American Dream.

So I was well aware that I was dealing with a prodigious South Indian polymath, omni-directional and blessed with seemingly illimitable energy. I was reminded that this graduate of both the Wharton School of Business and the legendary Indian Institute of Management was a man of constant surprises. And—as was the case again when I read his book—I was humbled to realize that I could never tell where he'd be a moment later.

Yet listening to the haunting and passionate calls to (and from) the spirit he'd recorded opened a door very different from all the magic portals we'd seen at Google; suddenly I got a glimpse of the soul, ancient and classical and rooted, hidden within this most secular and cutting-edge of settings. Here, I thought, was one of Silicon Valley's most intriguing and essential pieces of wisdom: that technology is less important than the inner resources we bring to it. And that achievement is more about the means we apply to our lives than simply the ends. The music was celestially joyful, yet its effect was to usher us into a silent space within; the melodies on *Kirtan Lounge* were catchy and distinctive, but they wove me into a larger whole in which all sense of individual self dissolved.

If Googlers and their colleagues in the Valley are the unacknowledged legislators of tomorrow's mankind, I thought, we need people with this rich and humbled sense of something beyond our ideas and calculations, high achievers who know the value of surrender as much as of control. If people like Gopi are in fact the new millennium's first Masters of the Universe, let them be guided by a sense of mystery as much as mastery, of unknowingness and of everything we can't quantify as well as of everything we can.

Walking around the mega-screens and beach volley-ball courts of the Googleplex gave me a sense of the field on which our new rulers meet and play; but listening to the music gave me hope for something more lasting than even Google Maps or Google Glass. Google Vision, you could call it, through which engineers can work on not just our tools, but on the souls that put them to best use.

▼▲▼

As soon as I picked up the book you're now holding, I thought back to a man I've been talking to for more than 40 years, who has the clearest set of priorities, the health-iest set of values I've encountered, the 14th Dalai Lama. Traveling with him across for Japan for eight straight autumns recently, I repeatedly heard him note that the Internet is a perfect embodiment of the classic Buddhist image of "Indra's Net," the web of interconnectedness that reminds us that none of us exists inside a vacuum. Our destinies have always been intertwined, of course—we rely on the decisions and thoughtfulness of thousands of others just to navigate a road—but never has the "butterfly effect" been so visible and so widespread as today, when we are sometimes almost painfully conscious that a de-cision in Mountain View this afternoon will have effects in Beijing tonight—and an attack in Baghdad will be felt minutes later across the United States.

One thing that Gopi's story reminds me of is that someone whose roots lie in a tiny rice-growing village in southern India (and none of whose forebears had a pass-port when he was growing up) can now, thanks to glob-al communications, orbit the planet and rewire our lives; the other, more surprising truth is that the way he serves humanity, as high-flying Googler, is based to a large extent on his traditional moorings in rural Kerala.

I learned a lot from following my friend on the adventures he describes here, whether through the wisdom he passes on of Rabbi Balfour Brickner and Mahatma Gandhi, or through his tonic sense of the virtues of single-tasking. I got to meet a saleswoman for Clinique in Cyprus who comes from Zambia—and rejoices in the name of "Meekness"—just before I encountered a terrifically lucid explanation of how yoga breaks down a limiting (and limited) sense of separate self, and releases us to something higher, as an ice cube goes through different incarnations while never losing its fundamental essence.

I was moved by how often our author was brave enough to show himself lost, or at sea in a blizzard of information, a typically stumbling Everyman brought back to a realization that the universe may have plans for us much wiser than our own; I was startled—and envious—to find him in Antarctica (as well as Mongolia, The Gambia, Cyprus), all places I've never been, and to see how he could extract wisdom from a flight attendant's safety instructions. Again and again I felt that he was stitching hemispheres together, not only across the globe but within the self; reminding us that the head is only as good as its readiness to defer to the heart, and that some of the most important appointments we may make are with ourselves.

Most of all, I delighted in his sheer appetite for the world, his rare ability to "stay hungry, stay foolish," as Steve Jobs advised in his celebrated commencement address at Stanford; you can almost feel Gopi's delight in "a belief system of expanded possibilities" that allows his voracious consumption of experience to flow into his enthusiasm for his company. Though I've not always made my peace with our latest technologies—I try to live with as few distractions as possible, so I won't lose sight of what outlasts them—I'm always braced by his refusal to let machines get in the way of humanity. As Meister Eckhart had it 700 years ago, if the inner work is strong, the outer work will never be puny.

All my life, in fact, I've been thinking and writing about the very issue that Gopi addresses at the heart of this book, and I was amazed to see the central question of my destiny posed so directly at the center of his own: how do we hold on to a sense of perspective and proportion amidst the clamor and congestion of Times Square? His answer—all but irrefutable, I think—is to step into the spacious attentiveness that meditation opens up, as into a hushed and quiet Westin Hotel. Such calm is only a way station, perhaps, but even a few minutes there allows you to handle the crowds and the screens outside with greater clarity.

The Chief Evangelist for Brand Marketing at Google, I realized, is also an evangelist for the unmarketing that comes from thinking about service—and unbranding oneself, at some level, by seeing the self as nothing more than a drop in the ocean.

Perhaps I am predisposed to listen to the likes of Gopi; maybe I am more guided by my own Indian origins than I suppose. When I was 29, I left my 25th-floor office four blocks from Times Square to live in a single room on the back streets of Kyoto, Japan, without toilet or telephone or even bed. Twenty-eight years on, my wife and I share a two-room rented apartment in the middle of an anonymous Japanese suburb where we've lived happily for more than 20 years without car or bicycle or media. "You may depend on it," Thoreau wrote, as if to anticipate the

in-boxes I've been trying to unclutter, "that the poor fellow who walks away with the greatest number of letters,
proud of his extensive correspondence, has not heard
from himself this long while."

Yet what Gopi and many of his friends and colleagues
are trying to do, even more impressively, is ensure that
there is a space for Walden Pond even amidst the digital
wonders and blinking lights of the Google campus; and
that helping to advance technology and our sense of possibility comes from singing kirtans as much as from producing spreadsheets. It's no coincidence that Gopi has his
name written in Malayalam above his e-mail address and
that, as I write this, he and some fellow Googlers are off in
Nepal bringing all their resources to trying to rescue local
women from sex trafficking. Working on mind and working on matter are not mutually exclusive, but, in fact, part
of the same process, whereby each can enhance the other.

In this book, after all, what you'll meet is not a monk
advising us to sit still and find reasons for gratitude, to
extend trust to the universe and never forget what is larger
than ourselves; here is a former consultant for McKinsey
& Co. and busy traveling man who's speeding along the
freeway to the airport, but seldom forgets the value of in-
wardness in practice as much as in theory. Enjoying an
onstage conversation with Gopi at the Wisdom 2.0 conference on clarity and kindness in the digital age, visiting
Silicon Valley two other times that same month alone, I've
been most impressed to find that the people at the fore-
front of our technological revolution are often the ones
wisest about how technology cannot give us everything.

Reading Gopi's book gave me an exhilarated sense of
all the new possibilities that are remaking every human
life every second; but most of all, it recalled to me that

it's only somebody who knows the old who can put the new into perspective. The deepest kind of interconnection is the one that links the fast-moving Googler in California with the singer of ageless truths in his grandmother's ancestral home in Chittilamchery. Divisions, after all, are a creation of the mind; reality—as Gopi knows and so engagingly shows us—is an equal-opportunity employer that asks us only to give it time and proper attention. Once we do, its treasures will beautifully disclose themselves.

Pico Iyer
Nara, Japan
April 2015

Pico Iyer has recently delivered million-view TED talks on both stillness and travel and is the author of such long-selling books as Video Night in Kathmandu, The Lady and the Monk, *and* The Global Soul.

INTRODUCTION

There are 7.2 billion people in our human family. Of these, an estimated 3 billion are on the Internet. Already, more people have access to mobile phones (7 billion subscriptions worldwide) than have access to electricity or clean drinking water. What are we doing with this technology, and what is it doing to us?

My roots go back to a small rice-farming village called Chittilamchery in Kerala, southern India, where my grandparents were poor rice farmers. My mother grew up in that same village, and my father grew up in a small village 6.4 miles away. Both grew up without electricity or running water and received a very basic education from the village school. Modest at best. But their four children, my brother and my two sisters and I, went on to earn a combined ten college degrees, including two U.S. Ivy League MBAs, even though my parents had never set foot in America. What caused this social mobility in one generation? It was, very simply, access to information.

Today when I go back to Chittilamchery, the school where my mother studied looks just the same. But in that school and in thousands of similar schools around the world, kids with access to the Internet now can find the same amount of information as someone at

Harvard, Stanford, or the University of Pennsylvania. In an era where information is like oxygen, the Internet is leveling the playing field for humanity. Think of the learning this information ignites, the opportunities it creates, the lives it can truly change.

Living in Silicon Valley, working at Google, I'm surrounded by these amazing technologies. The technological explosion in Silicon Valley and in tech companies all over the world has made a huge difference in our lives at a rapid pace. But these technologies also have a tendency to drive us to distraction. The information coming at us is relentless. E-mails pour into our in-boxes at all times of the day. Status updates on social networks pull us into the rhythm of other people's lives. We have daily, weekly, monthly blogs to read, videos to watch, and reports to review. The relentless interruptions from these electronic devices can be overwhelming.

In the midst of all this advancement, we must remember that the most important technology we deal with is right here, inside us. It is our *inner-net,* our brain, our body, our mind, our breath, our consciousness—the set of personal technologies that we carry with us everywhere. For our inner technology to operate at peak performance, it needs periods of quiet; it needs periods of restoration and replenishment. Living consciously, living with full engagement, and working with well-developed sciences, such as yoga and meditation, drawn from the world's wisdom traditions—these are all ways by which we can touch and transform our inner technology, so that we can live in harmony and balance with the outer.

Some of the chapters in this book draw upon specific practices from wisdom traditions. Some focus on rituals (creating a daily gratitude list) and strategies (scheduling appointments with myself) that I've developed on my own. And some are reflections that have guided me in my attempt to live more consciously on this planet, reflections driven by being in a diverse set of experiences and environments, from Burning Man to the bottom of the world in Antarctica. You can read the chapters individually, of course, or you can read them sequentially, following the flow of Parts I through V, where I've used terms from outer technology to reflect the inner practice of conscious living—from "logging in" and engaging with the world, to optimizing your "system" so you can operate at peak performance, to gratefully embracing all you've signed up for in this life.

While I believe we need to regularly unplug from the Internet and plug into our inner-net, I'm not advocating unplugging from the outer world completely. Instead, I think it's important to integrate the two worlds in a way that works for you. In his article "Stay Connected" in the March 2012 issue of *Yoga Journal,* Allan Tilin quoted my good friend Soren Gordhamer, founder of Wisdom 2.0. "How do we live mindfully in a constantly connected age?" Soren asks. "Wisdom traditions have some piece of that answer. Technology has some piece of that answer. Those two worlds need to come together for us to find a full answer."

I have spent years living in two worlds. I was blessed to be born into a culture where practicing meditation, yoga, and mindfulness has been an integral part of people's daily lives for hundreds of years. When I was a teenager, two seminal events occurred: I was initiated into meditation by my guru Tara Devi, and I studied at the Sivananda Ashram in Neyyar Dam in Kerala,

India, to become a yoga teacher. I continue to incorporate those practices in my everyday life. At the same time, I now live in Silicon Valley and work in the fast-paced, warp-speed, hyperinnovative environment that is Google, the high-tech industry, and, increasingly, life in general.

On my way to work, I pass the perfect juxtaposition of my two worlds. On the side of Highway 101, the main artery through Silicon Valley, looms a huge statue of the Buddha. His back to the industrial park where he sits, he smiles at the harried tech workers hurrying to their jobs at Google and Facebook and Apple. I don't know if they even notice him. But the Buddha, not at all concerned whether he's being acknowledged or not, sits with a serene look on his face, holding his hand up, as though in blessing: *Go in peace, go slowly.*

There's an incongruity to it. A philosopher from 2,500 years ago who urged the middle path now sits along a traffic-clogged freeway ferrying people on their way to, most likely, build products and systems that will improve our lives and connect us to each other, yet also add to the frenzy and deluge of information we face in our accelerated lives. When I see the Buddha, in that brief second of turning my head, I'm reminded that I need to pause and reflect on something larger than the day's schedule that currently occupies my mind.

The world is always changing. Nothing stands still. In exploring both worlds in which I live, I'm always experimenting. Often my experiments reinforce the experiments of others—my meditation and yoga practices, 20-minute naps, mindful eating. I also experiment with ways to fit those rituals into my hectic life in the high-tech industry. I am incredibly grateful to have the opportunity to share these experiments with you. I hope that in the pages of this book you will find principles that it helps you to reflect upon, that my experiments will spark your own, and that you will develop your own ways to find your balance and live fully and joyfully in both your outer and your inner world.

PART I

LOG IN

Fifteen years ago, we could log in to the Internet only from our desktops. That was it. Now we can log in from anywhere. When we're on a plane waiting for takeoff, in a subway station waiting for a train, sitting in a park—we can log in. This doesn't mean we need to answer our phones every minute, respond to every e-mail, jump on every post, but we can stay connected. Just as we stay connected in our inner life. We don't just check in once a week at yoga class or during a retreat to Sedona. We stay logged in.

What about the popular idea that we can't fully experience the inner world if we're too caught up in the outer? There is a story in the *Bhagavad Gita* in which the warrior Arjuna looks across the battlefield and refuses to fight. He says, in effect, "My friends and cousins are in the other army. I can't battle them." And Krishna replies, "You must. In your role as a warrior, you need to battle and do so with honor." I think he is saying that this world is not to be avoided, but engaged. We must walk through doors when they open. Answer the phone. Respond to the mail. Log in.

BE THE BISON

"Ladies and gentlemen," the chairperson of the conference announced, "we have a distinguished speaker from Google with us today. Please welcome Gopi Kallayil."

Amid applause, I stepped onto the stage in front of some 400 attendees. I was all set to deliver my keynote address on "Technology for Greater Good" at the Wisdom 2.0 Conference to this audience of mostly senior citizens attending sessions on wisdom and aging. I knew my subject backward and forward, and with my Toastmasters training, I was perfectly at ease as I greeted them and pressed the clicker to advance to my first slide.

Nothing happened.

I had seen this problem before, so I wasn't concerned. "It will be just another thirty seconds," I told the audience, "and I'll be ready to start."

But still nothing happened. My computer was frozen solid. The mouse was dead. The keyboard was sulking. The cursor was not winking back at me. I began to feel a little anxious. "It will be just another *sixty* seconds," I said.

I rebooted my computer and heard that familiar, reassuring sound that a computer makes when starting. *Cha . . . chaaang . . .* It warms our hearts when we hear that sound. It reassures us that all is well in our life.

Except all was not well in my life on that stage. *Cha . . . chaaang* went my computer, and then it gasped and died. Three times I tried it. Three times it went *cha . . . chaaang* and sputtered and died again. With each *cha . . . chaaang* a small part of me died.

By this time I had been on the stage for nine minutes. I had not even started my talk. Nine minutes is a very long time when you are standing in front of 400 people. Now the audience was snickering. *Even the Google guy can't make his technology work for him.*

That was when I remembered the story of the American bison. This was a story my colleague Mike Nelson had told us at work. When we were in the midst of a challenging work situation, Mike pulled a buffalo nickel out of his pocket that he'd had for a long time. He intended to pass it along to his own children. The coin had an image of the American bison embossed on it. As we looked at Mike's coin, he told us this story from the American West about the American bison.

Mike's family is from Montana, where winter storms in the mountains and valleys are swift and brutal. When a storm approaches, the wind starts howling. Heavy snow covers the ground. All the wild animals flee the storm. Except the bison. The bison is the only animal that will turn toward the storm, lean into it, and walk to meet it. It knows instinctively that if it does this, it will be out of the storm sooner. This is why Native Americans call the bison "Faces the Storm."

As I stood on that stage, with my presentation in shambles, a storm was rapidly approaching me. Mike Nelson's story had prepared me for it. I chose to be the bison. I walked into the storm.

I stepped to the center of the stage. "Ladies and gentlemen," I said, "I came here to talk about the amazing technologies we build at Google. But the most important technology we use in our lives is right here—our body, our breath, our brain. Let me show you how we can use this technology most effectively when challenged by life's problems. Let me teach you a small breathing and mindfulness technique I am using right now to manage this situation up here on the stage."

From that beginning, I gave an impromptu keynote on how to manage our inner technology when our outer technology fails and creates a problem we don't expect and can't immediately solve. The audience had stopped snickering. I felt a tremendous sense of support and empathy from them. I told them to breathe a little more slowly, a little more deeply; to notice whatever was arising in their bodies and minds with no judgment, but lean into the feeling. If it was a feeling of panic as I was experiencing a few moments ago, that was okay too. I told them to lean into the feeling and walk toward it just as the bison do. All of a sudden, the feeling is no longer intimidating, and soon enough it passes just like the storm as the bison walk through it.

When I finished speaking, they gave me a standing ovation.

We all want certainty in our lives. But the only thing I am certain of about your life is that there is no certainty. At any point in time you may come face-to-face with a small irritant, a large problem, or even a full-scale life catastrophe. It may come in your work, in your finances, or in your relationships. When that happens, you can choose to be the bison. Turn toward the storm. Walk toward it. Walk *through* it.

Embracing whatever life places in front of us—that is full engagement. That is the suchness of life. That is the juiciness of life. That is the fullness of life.

FLOAT TO THE TOP

When I am at a party, the question I dislike the most is "What do you do?" I often challenge the other person by responding, "I live joyously and consciously. That is what I do." But the very idea of living joyously and consciously is hard to grasp, let alone sustain, amid the demands of today's fast-paced life.

I get at least 200 or 300 e-mails a day, each one a data fragment asking me to respond in some fashion. My grandfather, farming his rice field in a small village in India, probably had to respond to four or five pieces of communication a day. For him, once the sun went down and the cattle were back in the shed, the rhythm of life changed. Not in Silicon Valley, where I work—the rhythm is 24/7. There is no dial to turn down and say, "I want a bit less of it." So you have to accept that these are the conditions you are choosing to have, and then ask, "In the midst of this, how can I be peaceful, happy, and content?"

The fact is that technology is like fire. Ever since we discovered fire and knew how to harness it, we've found it exceptionally useful. You can cook your food with fire; you can melt and blow glass with it. But if you misuse it, you can burn yourself or raze an entire city to the ground. Technology is a powerful tool—but whether you use the tool to be productive or destructive, to live with peace or chaos, is up to you.

At Google, where I work, we are building amazing technologies like self-driving cars, Android phones, and Google Maps. But to live a truly conscious life, we need to connect with our inner technology—and there are simple steps you can take to log on to your inner-net, starting right now.

Communities of employees at Google—"Googlers"— organize themselves into groups that center on different interests. We have Gayglers, Jewglers, and Carpooglers. I started a group for Yoga called Yoglers with just one student—but word spread and it has become a larger program across many Google offices. When you practice yoga, you're asked to bring your complete 100 percent awareness to your body and your breath. If you practice regularly, you stay more aware, and you make choices driven by that. The quality of your interactions improves. You stop checking your e-mail when someone is talking to you. You become a more conscious human being.

Yoga to me can be practiced all the time, like meditation. Every single moment of every day, I try to be mindful, whether I am engaging with a janitor, a chef, an engineer, or a marketing colleague. I do set aside time for specific practices, and for the Yoglers class I teach, but in truth, every moment of every day is my inner work.

What if you don't have a yoga or meditation program at your work? It's simple. Go book a conference room. Sit, close your eyes, start meditating. It doesn't matter if only one person shows—or if no one does. If you sit there for 60 seconds and watch your breath, you have just started a meditation program. You don't need a budget or resources.

Someone just needs to step forward and do it. Someone—perhaps *you.*

What's essential to realize is that you don't need to withdraw from the outer world in order to create a peaceful space in your inner world. Some people think they can find peace and avoid conflict—like, say, the stress of being passed over for a promotion—by going to live at a monastery or an ashram. But I have been to many ashrams and seen that these issues follow you. You think that the director of the ashram should have promoted you to be senior teacher! We tend to think, *I have my work life. Then I have my spiritual life.* But the same person with the same body shows up everywhere.

The challenge, of course, is to engage the world without getting entangled. A lovely metaphor that I grew up with in India is that of the beautiful lotus flower. It always floats on top of the water, even though the roots are mired in the mud below. When water falls on a lotus leaf, it gently flows off like dewdrops. The message in the metaphor is that we can be involved in life and work without being mired in it. We can let our problems roll off us. We can float to the top.

TRAVEL THE WORLD

"The world is a book," said Saint Augustine, "and those who do not travel read only a page."

When I was growing up in Kerala, India, I was one of those reading only a page—or a paragraph. I had never traveled outside India. No one in my family had. We barely knew anyone who had. People I knew did not have passports. It just wasn't done.

But in Thiruvananthapuram, the town where I went to high school, I would go to the main public library, and there I saw books that opened up a new world to me. I spent hours poring in awe over a volume on the South Pacific islands with illustrations of people and places such as I had never imagined. Today, images like this are accessible from all over the world at the click of a mouse or a remote, but remember that this was before the Internet, and our home did not even have a TV. These places called out to me, and the strange names resonated deeply with me: Tokelau and Tonga, Futuna and Niue.

I was the first in my family to get a passport when I was all of 18. My parents fought it. "Why do you need a passport?" they pressed. "Why would you want to go to other countries? We don't know anyone in those countries." But I persisted. I knew there was more to the world than just what I saw around me, and I wanted to go out into it. "We need sometimes to escape into open solitudes," said George Santayana in his *Philosophy of Travel,* "in order to sharpen the edge of life, to taste hardship, and to be compelled to work desperately for a moment at no matter what." I wanted to sharpen the edge. I wanted to work desperately for a moment.

Today, I have traveled through 54 countries and all seven continents—from Iceland near the Arctic Circle all the way down to the barren wastes of Antarctica—and I am more awed than ever at the huge and diverse world we occupy.

Some years ago, I came across another book that transported me in much the same way. Published by Lonely Planet, *The Travel Book* is a journey through literally every country in the world, and it would become my touchstone for my own journeys.

The world in its pages is viewed with a pleasing kind of egalitarianism: the United States and the UK get the same two pages, with half a dozen pictures and a block of text, as do Cote d'Ivoire and Togo. Starting from Afghanistan, Albania, and Algeria and working my way to Zambia and Zimbabwe, I felt a growing sense of wonder as dramatically different countries followed each other. Belgium after Belarus, Martinique after Marshall Islands, Tuvalu after Turks and Caicos, Virgin Islands after Vietnam. Countries were mysteriously handcuffed through history and heritage that now linked their names through the English alphabet, barely hiding a deeper connection shared by humans. In this book, Pakistan found itself between Oman and Palau, but that was because the British partitioned India; otherwise the people of Pakistan would have found themselves in the book between Iceland and Indonesia. And the images were haunting—Gitaga dancers leaping in the air, volcanic plugs in Rhumsiki, herders following a flock of sheep in Cotopaxi, donkeys picking their way down cobble steps on Santorini, and a bejeweled Bedouin girl smiling beneath a florid headscarf.

I flipped through the pages excitedly, stopping at some of the countries I had been to—Australia, the Czech Republic, French Polynesia, Gambia, Israel, Malaysia, Mongolia, Vatican City—and flagging the places I still want to go: Bhutan, the Dominican Republic, Morocco, Panama, Pitcairn Islands, Tibet, Turkey, Vanuatu . . . places that I knew would open my eyes wider still.

As the book's jacket says, "Ever since our first, faltering upright steps, humankind has traveled. Everywhere is migration, exploration, pursuit. Terrible things have been caused by this restlessness, but it is also the source of much that is extraordinary and wonderful." Travel makes you aware of the tremendous diversity and difference in our world and the humans who live in it—and at the same time, in a paradoxical way, of how alike we are. Everyone wants to be happy. Everyone wants a sense of security. Everywhere, people take care of their families and take care of each other. But hearing this is one thing, and experiencing it on your own is something else. It changes your perspective in amazing ways.

As soon as you set foot in a new place, you are outside your normal frame of reference. The infrastructure, the language, the look of things, the way things work—all these are unfamiliar, to a greater or lesser degree. You learn to travel with wonder and a sense of exploration while at the same time honoring each place you go, treating it as sacred and leaving no trace of your passage behind. And somehow, in paying attention to what is new all around you, you become newly alert and present to your own life.

"We travel, initially, to lose ourselves," my good friend Pico Iyer once famously wrote, "and we travel, next, to find ourselves." Pico is my favorite writer and also leads a charmed life I have aspired after, splitting his time each year between rural Japan, where he lives with his wife; Dharamsala, India, where the Dalai Lama lives in exile; the New Camaldoli Hermitage on the Big Sur coast in California; and Santa Barbara, where his mother lives. And in between he could be in any number of places around the world. I once e-mailed him from a train going through Alappuzha, in Kerala, India, and he was getting off a boat in Vietnam. I was on a slow boat to Turku in Finland and he was at the Jaipur writers' festival. He seems to float effortlessly between Wau in Sudan, Jaffna in Sri Lanka, and Sucre in Bolivia.

"We travel to open our hearts and eyes," Pico's famous passage continues, "and learn more about the world than our newspapers will accommodate. We travel to bring what little we can, in our ignorance and knowledge, to those parts of the globe whose riches are differently dispersed. And we travel, in essence, to become young fools again—to slow time down and get taken in, and fall in love once more."

Knock on the Door

Thirteen years ago, I wrote a list of 100 things I wanted to do in my life. And number 36 read: "Meet the Dalai Lama in person." Even though I had never seen him.

Soon after, opportunities started presenting themselves almost magically to attend his teaching. I walked into the back of a bookstore and saw a poster announcing that he was speaking nearby the following week. I heard him speak in unlikely places—an indoor stadium in Sydney, the Shoreline Amphitheatre and Greek Theatre near San Francisco, the basketball stadium at Stanford University. Places where I was used to seeing the Stanford Cardinals, Coldplay, and Sigur Rós, not the world's most famous Buddhist monk.

But as I returned to the Google office from the talk at Stanford, it struck me that I had not done much about my goal to meet the Dalai Lama in person and did not know where to start. Perhaps a good first step would be simply to ask someone?

The first person I ran into after I had that thought was my colleague and good friend Chade-Meng Tan, a famous Google engineer who had an affiliation with meditation research and projects that I knew were of interest to the Dalai

Lama. I told him that I wanted to meet the Dalai Lama in person. Deadpan, he replied, "Sure, that can be arranged. What are you doing two weeks from now?" Amazingly, he was serious. He went on, "Can you be in Dharamsala in India in two weeks?" He told me to speak to a friend of his, Lama Tenzin Dhonden, global peace emissary for the Dalai Lama, who was arranging a meeting between His Holiness and a few people from the United States.

But Lama Tenzin was traveling and unreachable. Should I go anyway? Even as I was wondering if I should rearrange my life for a week to take this trip with no guarantee that I would get an audience, I ran into Jeremiah, another Google engineer, in the locker room. He said, "If you don't go, thirty years from now you will have no recollection of what you did this week at work. If you do go, you will remember and cherish this meeting for the rest of your life."

I knew he was right, but I still hesitated—until my mentor, Stuart Newton, sent me over the tipping point. "You asked the universe and it has opened the door," he said. "Now you must walk through it." Two weeks later I was on a plane to Dharamsala.

Right up until a few hours before the meeting, I did not know if it would happen; I had not heard from Lama Tenzin. When I did get an e-mail from him, while I was in transit through the Hong Kong airport, he wrote that usually they need two weeks to confirm the final guest list for the day, complete security checks, and so on, and I was giving them only 48 hours from the time I sent my passport information. But this is exactly the kind of thing I am willing to travel 36 hours halfway around the world for: just to show up and knock on a door in the hope that it might open.

After three days of hanging around the Dalai Lama's monastery in Dharamsala, I received confirmation that I would indeed meet him. Jeremiah was right: it will always be one of the most cherished memories of my life. I spent 45 minutes in a personal audience with His Holiness, listening as his conversation ranged from compassion to human values to happiness to neuroplasticity and mental training. It was so moving and his humanity so touching that when I said good-bye and thank you, there were tears in my eyes. The Dalai Lama gave me a *katta* (a white cloth with Tibetan prayers inscribed) as a blessing that I brought back with me and hung above my desk so that it would rain blessings on the entire team of colleagues I work with.

I think it worked, because about a year later an e-mail winged its way from the Dalai Lama's office to my Google colleague Shailesh in India and then on to my colleagues Vic in the United States and Marvin in Korea before landing finally in my in-box. It expressed an interest that the office of the Dalai Lama had in the product I was working on—Google+ —and it started me noodling some ideas on a piece of paper. One of them was to put the Dalai Lama together with Archbishop Desmond Tutu in a Google Hangout and allow thousands of people to view it live on the Internet. I told a few colleagues about this random and crazy idea and left it at that.

Five days later, a Googler from South Africa, Jonathan, called me at home at one in the morning. I had never met him before, and yet he made the following request: "The Arch's [Archbishop Desmond Tutu's] birthday is coming up this Saturday, and his friend the Dalai Lama was to be the main guest, delivering a talk on peace and compassion. He has applied for a visa but hasn't been granted one yet, so the Arch's office has asked if we could use technology to find a solution."

The next morning, I sat discussing the possibilities with Loren, the product manager for Google Hangouts, in our usual place under the *katta*. Five hours later, Loren was on a 33-hour journey to South Africa. What was remarkable was that Loren had never before traveled outside the United States. He had gotten a passport just a few months earlier, thinking it might be a good idea to start traveling internationally. A dozen of us from Google in four different countries around the world swung into action—we had just 60 hours to make it happen. Jonathan had knocked on a door, and it had opened.

So, a mere seven days after I had put my original intention down on paper, the Dalai Lama stepped in front of a Google Hangouts window on a computer in his house in Dharamsala, India. Half a world away, Archbishop Desmond Tutu stepped in front of another Hangouts window on a computer at the University of the Western Cape, in Cape Town, South Africa. He waved at his dear friend and spiritual brother and chuckled. "I can see you clearly!"

Leading up to the event there was high pressure for everyone as unexpected problems cropped up. The power went out 15 minutes before the Hangout, after which a South African Secret Service Agent was dispatched to guard the site's switchboard. And power in the main undersea Internet cable to South Africa went out—for reasons I don't know—just 20 minutes after the event had finished.

But the Hangout itself was flawless. From their offices, living rooms, and bedrooms, thousands of people watched this historic dialogue unfold live. The previous 13 Dalai Lamas had hardly traveled beyond Tibet. And now here was the 14th Dalai Lama chatting with Desmond Tutu, and it felt as if it were happening in your house. In a mere seven days, a crazy idea I put on a piece of paper had transformed itself from intention to manifestation. It makes me think: What else might be achieved? What other doors might open if we only knock?

SISTER MADONNA

On a beautiful summer day in May, I was riding my bicycle down a leafy Palo Alto road, one of the roads around Xerox PARC. That was the road that my coach at the Silicon Valley Triathlon Club had chosen for a training ride for us beginning triathletes. Then suddenly I was lying on my back on the pavement, wondering, *What . . . just . . . happened?*

What had happened was that I'd hit a pothole, sending me and my bike flying. That was my first attempt to train for a triathlon, and, yes, I was off to a *crashing* start. But what do you do when you crash? Do you look around to make sure nobody was watching, or do you get back in the saddle, determined to accomplish your goal?

Before I tell you what I did, let me tell you a little about the world of triathlons. A triathlon consists of three sports—swimming, cycling, and running. And the most grueling of triathlons is the IRONMAN: you swim 2.6 miles in a lake, you cycle for 112 miles, and finally you run a full marathon, 26.2 miles. Who comes up with these events? And who competes in them? Professionals, right?

Wrong! My most inspiring triathlete is not a professional athlete at all. Sister Madonna Buder, an 84-year-old Catholic nun, has raced more than 300 triathlons, some of them IRONMAN distances, and become the oldest person—man or woman—ever to complete an IRONMAN. She started when she turned 50 because a priest told her that exercise was good for body, mind, and spirit. If somebody told you that, would you start a walking program, or would you start training for the most grueling competition you could find? Sister Madonna did not take the easy route.

I had heard about Sister Madonna—nicknamed the Iron Nun—from Tony Robbins in one of his motivational programs. Inspired by her, I joined a triathlon training program, and in my first week I crashed. I was discouraged at first, and I thought about quitting. Then I wondered, *What would Sister Madonna do?* She crashed several times in her racing career. Once she broke her elbow, clavicle, and jaw. She took a year off and then did two IRONMANs the next year.

Following Sister Madonna's example, I decided to stick with the program. So I told myself, *It is not my fault that I crashed. It is the bike's fault. I need a new bike.* I went to buy a brand-new triathlon bike and had the shock of my life. It cost me almost a month's mortgage.

A month later I was driving down Highway 101 with the bike strapped to the back of my car. I looked in my rearview mirror—*and there was no bike.* The bike had fallen on the freeway and was bouncing like a basketball. Cars were dribbling and swerving. I sat there feeling helpless and terrified, waiting for the inevitable multicar pileup. When the drama ended, there was no pileup, but my new bike—my one-month's mortgage payment—was six pieces of useless metal. A foreclosure!

Undaunted, I borrowed a friend's bike and registered for a short beginner's triathlon.

At the starting line on the day of the event, I stared nervously at the lake, as swimming is my Achilles' heel. I grew up in an Indian state, Kerala, population 30 million, number of swimming pools—one! I learned to swim subsequently but felt safe only in my bathtub.

The race started and for the first time in my life I was swimming in a lake. It was chaotic, with more than 1,000 bodies splashing around me. Fifteen yards into the water I panicked. The water was dark, deep, and dangerous. There was kelp all over my face. I was swallowing water. Clearly I was drowning. But the thought that was going through my head in that instant was *Gosh! I have a dinner party tonight.* These are the thoughts that go through your head when you are drowning. I was thinking, *The guests will arrive and find the house dark. Three days later they will find out that the party did not take place because Gopi was dead.* Just then a lifeguard pulled me out of the water. Now I was really, really ready to abandon my triathlon goals. Again I thought of Sister Madonna. She would not have given up.

So with a new resolve, I jumped right back into my training. That Saturday I rode 30 miles on my bike without crashing, on Sunday I ran 10 miles without stumbling, on Tuesday I swam for an hour without drowning.

We humans achieve the most miraculous things when role models inspire us. The role model for middle distance runners is Roger Bannister. Before the 1950s, it was believed that no human being could run a mile in under four minutes. In 1954 Bannister chose to believe differently and became the first human to run a mile in under four minutes. That same year 31 other athletes did it. The next year more than 300 athletes did it. What changed? It was not that the Nike of that era had introduced a new pair of running shoes. For all these athletes, Roger Bannister had set the example of stretching past the old limits.

The truth is that there are no limitations you can't push past; the only limits on you are the ones you place there yourself. And you can find inspiration in the most unlikely places. Sister Madonna, the 84-year-old triathlete nun, is proof: you never know where your teachers are going to come from.

Along my triathlon route I reached a powerful realization: there is something in the human psyche that shifts when you come across someone who has accomplished a goal you are pursuing. There's something that changes at a subconscious level, an almost mystical level, that propels you toward the goal. And the role model you find does not even have to have accomplished the exact same goal; all it has to be is something you can draw a parallel from. This is how Roger Bannister inspired thousands of people to break the four-minute-mile barrier. And this is how Sister Madonna inspired me to complete my first small triathlon.

What goals have you been putting off for tomorrow, a tomorrow that may never come? Change careers? Travel around the world? Or just teach your dog to roll over? Every human being is gifted with the power to imagine, set goals, and aspire to reach them. Go ahead. Step into the field of all possibilities; fully engage the world in a way you might not have thought you could. Just the act of exploring, itself, is a big part of life. As you explore, find a role model who has done what you aspire to do. Keep in mind that you may find him or her in the most unlikely place. And if you crash in the beginning, remember your Sister Madonna. I promise you, each time you will rise.

BORDERS

From the sky Cyprus looks like a lotus leaf floating in the azure-blue Mediterranean basin. With just over a million people, it is smaller than the San Francisco Bay Area in both size and population. When my plane lands at Larnaca International Airport, the ground crew wheels in a staircase for us to disembark. I know instantly that I have arrived in a place where I can truly get away. From Banjul in The Gambia to Ulan Bator in Mongolia, from Thiruvananthapuram in India to Liberia in Costa Rica, that test has always worked well. The reassuring sight of a stairwell being wheeled in means you will get off in a place very different from the business cities around the world—Chicago, Frankfurt, Shanghai, Dubai—that seem to look and feel more like each other all the time.

Surrounded by Greece, Turkey, Syria, Lebanon, Israel, and Egypt, Cyprus is a testimony to the aphorism that geography is destiny. Over the centuries, invaders, settlers, and immigrants have come through—the Greeks, Romans, Byzantines, Lusignans, Genoese, Venetians, Ottomans, British, Turks—each leaving their stamp on Cyprus. Reading about its history and all the occupation evokes Churchill's definition of history in my mind: "One damn thing after another."

Today, the island is split into an uneasy, disconcerting two parts—a Greek side and a Turkish side—by a divide that has seared the soul of a nation. I walk through downtown Lefkosia, the capital, to the Ledra Street border crossing. Ledra Street, a pedestrian-only street, is a lovely medley of cafés, music stores, and boutiques—but at the end of the street I walk across the "Green Line" past a sign that says "Last Divided Capital in the World." As I leave the Republic of Cyprus side, another sign welcomes me to the Turkish Republic of Northern Cyprus. The very existence of this country I am now standing in defies logic; it is recognized by just one other country, Turkey.

In 1963, the British occupied Cyprus. In response to communal disturbances between Greek and Turkish Cypriots, the British military took a green pen and drew a line on the military map, creating the Green Line that divided the city. I like to imagine that they reached into a colonial handbook and thumbed through it for the entry that said, "How to govern local population effectively." And there, instructions would have read, "Take map, take green pen, draw line across map, tell population to shift from one side of the line to another along tribal, ethnic, or religious lines."

In 1974, after military activity involving Greece and Turkey, the whole of Cyprus was divided into Greek and Turkish parts and the Green Line now extended across the entire island. Another partition tragedy for humanity repeated as hundreds of ordinary Greek and Turkish Cypriots had to uproot themselves and abandon their homes, farms, and livelihoods. Forced to cross over to the other side of the Green Line, they had to start their lives over.

I grew up in an India that had been similarly divided, splintering finally into three—India, Bangladesh, and Pakistan—a division that is still simmering to this day.

In Palestine and the Arabian Gulf, in North Africa, in North Korea and South Korea, the drive to "reorganize" along cultural or ethnic lines has torn apart populations, communities, and even families. With the heartache this creates, you might think that we would learn from our mistakes, but we don't—and, as George Santayana said, those who cannot learn from the past are doomed to repeat it.

What's interesting is that we are the only species that seems to want to do this. Animals don't do it; there's no fence across the Serengeti, no rule that says these wildebeest must live on this side and those elephants on the other. The earth is all of a piece to them. As it once was to us: the concept of borders is relatively new in human history. Pleistocene man did not have to pass a checkpoint to cross the Bering land bridge. Even Columbus sailed into the New World without so much as a visa stamp. As I remember the story, when Portuguese explorer Vasco da Gama arrived in Kozhikode (where I attended middle school) in the year 1498, the local king did not ask him for his visa but instead welcomed him to dinner. Of course, that led to the opening of European trade routes to India and eventually to 450 years of European domination of India. That was one dinner party that ended badly. And the lines that divide us today are usually drawn by a few individuals in power; the person on the ground, gazing through the fence, doesn't want the barrier. People mostly want to be together.

I am walking around Lefkosia's old city, which is surrounded by Venetian walls that from the top look like a snowflake or a sliced-open grenade. The Venetians built the walls in 1570 to keep the feared Ottomans out. The bastions were named after wealthy Venetian merchants who paid for the walls in a clever fund-raising model long before Harvard and Wharton learned to name their buildings after rich alums. Well, the Ottomans arrived three years after the walls were built, scaled the walls, took over Lefkosia, and stayed for 300 years. Another reminder that walls don't really keep anyone out.

In our times, the Green Line divided people from their friends and families for 29 years. Then, in 2008, the borders were abruptly opened by Rauf Denktas, the leader of the Turkish Cypriots. It was like the fall of the Berlin wall, with emotional scenes as people from both sides crossed over to see for themselves what life was like on the other side, in some cases traveling back to homes and friends they had left behind.

Cypriots today can cross the Green Line freely. Driving us around the old city is Ahmet, a Turkish Cypriot with a handlebar mustache, who bikes across the international border every day to come to work and drives a quaint school bus that looks as if it could be from the 1960s. I almost look around to see if beat poets and hipsters Allen Ginsberg, Jack Kerouac, and Wavy Gravy are on the bus. Ahmet tells me that he used to be a truck driver, driving tractor trailers from Finland to Bangladesh in marathon 20-day trips across all the central Asia "stans," plus Iran, Pakistan, and Afghanistan. *"Anda, Kela, Aap Khana Khawo,"* he tells me, using the few Hindi words he remembers from his trips, and guffaws loudly. I laugh, too, delighted by his joy and his gracious, nonsensical sentence: "Eggs, bananas—please, have some food."

Evie, a tour guide, is showing me through the old city. At one point she leads me to the border that separates the two sides of Cyprus. The watchtowers set up by the UN forces are now deserted. The forces are long gone since peace came. An elderly Cypriot gentleman comes out to greet us. His house backs up against the border. He probably grew up and lived all his life in this house till one day someone drew the Green Line across his backyard and arrived with rolls of barbed wire to prove it. Beyond the barbed-wire fence behind his house is a no-man's-land where houses, schools, hotels sit dilapidated and abandoned, out of bounds so that no one will step on a land mine.

Evie herself is a refugee across the border. Her family were wealthy farmers on the northern side. Suddenly history came calling. They abandoned their orange orchards and everything else they had and were forced to hit the "reset" button on their life. The border is open now, but Evie has not gone back. The memories are too haunting.

People want to be together, and walking through Lefkosia and traveling around Cyprus, it strikes me that we are finding ways. The modern-day waves of immigrants have filled the city with human stories with none of the clinical coldness of statistical tables. I find them everywhere. The Cameroonian sales clerk in the music store who helps me pick contemporary Cypriot music by Anna Vissi and Alkinoos Ioannides. Basheer from Bangladesh, who is a student and also mans a news kiosk, and loans me his cell phone to call a taxi. Meekness from Zambia, who staffs the Clinique counter at the airport, advising newly rich and badly sunburned Russians going home after their holiday in the sun on how to care for their skin. Pepe from India, who provides home care to an elderly Cypriot woman. The beautiful Hungarian waitress who shares a taxi with me and discusses the

Paulo Coelho book she is reading. The Nepali waiters who scurry around the seafood restaurant in Ayia Napa. Yannis, the former professional football player from Georgia, who arrived to play for a local team until his bad knees killed his football career; now he drives a taxi. The Sri Lankan nanny who takes care of the two-year-old brother of Diamondis, the psychology student at the University of Cyprus I meet during a shared ride. Each story is rich in its detail of economic migration, cultural displacement, opportunity, and hope.

But it occurs to me that the walls are coming down fastest of all in the virtual world, where more and more of us work, play, and connect. Where you can come across an amazing video on YouTube—an Israeli keyboardist and composer, Idan Reichel, and a Malian singer and guitarist, Vieux Farka Toura, collaborating to produce incredibly beautiful music that anyone anywhere in the world with an Internet connection can experience.

Governments put up fences with signs saying you can't travel to the other side—but the Internet jumps the fence. Borders are irrelevant in a world where information—and knowledge, stories, opinions, photographs, family moments, all of human experience—can fly around the world at the click of a mouse. You can see a face across a border; with language tools and translation software, you can even talk with someone whose language you don't understand.

Where is this all leading? To a point, I think, where we are questioning whether we need passports and visas to cross the green lines that carve up our planet. Or should we be working toward a world, 100 or 200 years from now, where we can travel freely wherever we want— where the earth is all of a piece? Where we connect and engage without impediments, where our world expands and our lives become so much richer? Except for human beings, every living being on the planet has no concept of borders and freely roams the earth. Perhaps humans need that kind of expansiveness too.

ORDINARY PEOPLE CAN HAVE AN EXTRAORDINARY IMPACT

Some 7.2 billion people make up our human family. Half of them live on $3 a day. Less than what we pay *for one cup of gourmet coffee.* Several of these live in my home village in India—Chittilamchery. And one of those people with very modest means whom I had never even met taught me that ordinary people, with limited resources, can have an extraordinary impact on the lives of others.

It all started with my parents. They grew up in Chittilamchery, without electricity, running water, or a college education. In one generation the family's fortunes shifted. My parents worked hard and created the circumstances for their four children to earn advanced degrees. My parents were just ordinary people.

I learned that lesson again from Oseola McCarty. Former President Bill Clinton had come to Google to speak and had given out copies of his book *Giving.* In the book, Clinton inspires the reader with the understanding that each of us can have an impact. To make his point, he goes on to introduce us to unsung heroes of giving. When I read in *Giving* that Oseola McCarty had created a scholarship at the University of Southern Mississippi, I thought, *Surely she must be a very wealthy woman.* Well, Oseola dropped out of school when she was 12 to care for her sick aunt. And for the next 75 years the only job she had was washing and ironing other people's clothes. Oseola McCarty was a washerwoman. She was frugal—didn't subscribe to a newspaper, walked everywhere she went, and saved her modest income in a bank. When she turned 87, she asked her bank manager how much money she had in her account. He answered, "Three hundred thousand dollars." I imagine she must have said something like "Son, there are no shopping malls on the way to heaven. I want to create a scholarship so that girls from poor families can go to college."

When news of Oseola's decision was made public, local leaders funded an endowment in her honor, increasing her gift's reach still more. Before she died four years later, USM's most famous donor received acclaim and honors including the Presidential Citizens Medal—the United States' highest civilian award—and honorary doctorates from USM and Harvard. Oseola McCarty was an ordinary person, and her resources at the outset were certainly limited, and yet she made an extraordinary impact on her world.

Have you ever wondered if you could have an impact like that on others too? I did, sitting in a coffee shop. The barista yelled out, "Gopi, your grande caramel cinnamon chocolate Frappuccino is ready. And it is fat-free." I knew that only the fat was "free," and it struck me that it was more abundance than many of the people I knew back in Chittilamchery would enjoy that entire day. So I wondered—could I sacrifice a few cups of coffee and make a big impact?

I found my answer in Kiva, a San Francisco–based organization that allows ordinary people, like most of us, to give microloans to women in the Third World who are starting small businesses.

That same day, I made my first loan online—for the princely sum of $25. The entrepreneur who received it was Ngô Thi Chung, a 54-year-old woman living in Trung Giã village, Vietnam, starting a farm supplies business. She needed a loan of $1,200, and I wondered how my $25 could help. But never underestimate the power of people working together. In four hours, several others had made modest loans of their own and she had her $1,200.

Next month, I gave another loan to Esther Laboso, a 46-year-old widow with five children living in Kericho, Kenya, who was starting a grain store. The following month it was a fisherwoman in Peru, and then a tailor in Pakistan. I was hooked. This was much better than a grande caramel cinnamon chocolate Frappuccino.

Recently, I connected with friends from high school. The lovely Lakshmi, the one from our class who was voted most likely to succeed, asked, "Gopi, where are you these days? What are you doing?" And I, who was voted most likely to join the circus, replied: "I am an international banker. I finance entrepreneurs around the world."

A few months ago Kiva sent me an e-mail. Esther, Ngô Thi, and the other women I had given loans to were building successful, profitable businesses and repaying their loans. It was less important that my loan had been repaid. I was proud of the fact that these women were telling the world, "We do not want charity. We are confident business owners." These women had found a sense of dignity.

And I was experiencing for myself the lesson that I first learned from my parents, that ordinary people with limited resources can have an extraordinary impact on the lives of others.

Perhaps you're inspired by these stories but still skeptical that this truth could ever apply to you. *Can I, an ordinary person with limited resources, really have an extraordinary impact on someone else's life?* Yes, you can, starting today. I learned this from my parents, from Oseola McCarty, and through my work with Esther Laboso and Ngô Thi Chung. Start with a microloan of $25 or a program of your choice.

There are plenty of options. Heifer International, for example, gives gifts of livestock to people in the Third World. (My grandparents had a single cow that provided milk for the whole family and was treasured.) A gift of a goat to the Biira family in a Ugandan village led to the mother selling goat's milk and sending all her kids to school—and, as required by the program, passing on a baby goat to another family to pay it forward. Any of us could easily gift a goat or a pig or a chicken or even a portion of a larger animal (in partnership with other donors) to a family.

As Clinton says in his book, "We all have the capacity to do great things." And we can do it with whatever resources we have on hand. Ordinary people, making an extraordinary impact.

THE ICE CUBE AND THE OCEAN

The purpose of yoga is contained in the meaning of the word *yoga* itself. I find that kind of self-referential encapsulation—or "recursive," we would say as an inside joke among my computer-science-loving classmates at university—quite beautiful.

Translated from Sanskrit into English, *yoga* simply means to join or achieve union. Join what? Join the individual consciousness to the universal consciousness. Or join our sense of self to the sense of something out there that is larger than ourselves no matter what label you are comfortable with—source, energy, consciousness, universe, God, Brahman.

And, according to yoga philosophy, the purpose of yoga, in fact the very purpose of life, is to achieve this union. Why should this matter? Why should you care? Yoga philosophy goes on to explain that a good portion of our problems—suffering, dissonance, and disillusionment—stems from a sense of separation, a sense of false identification, and a sense of limitation. I had heard some version of this in the trainings and lectures I received over the years. But it took me many years of reflection before I began to understand the essence of this wisdom. I explain it best to my students using the analogy of an ice cube.

An ice cube is a translucent piece of solid matter at zero degrees centigrade composed of frozen water molecules and with a specific shape. If the ice cube could talk, it would say something like this, "Hello, my name is Cool Ice, and I belong to the Ice Cube species. I am one cubic inch in size, always at zero degrees centigrade, a bit translucent, and I don't change my shape or dimension. If you were to raise the temperature, I would simply melt and cry, nay, die."

If you were to point out to the ice cube the flowing water in the Amazon River or a puff of steam rising up to become a cloud, the ice cube would respond, "I am extremely envious, but I simply could not flow like the mighty Amazon river or float freely like a white cloud. Those are not the intrinsic properties of the ice cube. I could not aspire to have that kind of formlessness or flow."

Yoga philosophy argues that we are in the same state as the ice cube. We are bounded and limited by our sense of false identification with our limited self around us. Our jobs, our bodies, our wealth, our possessions, our neighborhoods, and our social status define us. They give us our sense of identity and, more tragically, trap us in it.

This in turn leads to a sense of separation. The people we see around us are seen as distinct and separate from us. They have different jobs, bodies, wealth, possessions, neighborhoods, social status. And from this sense of separation, we start making comparisons that are the source of our unhappiness and suffering. Suffering in the forms of jealousy, greed, acquisitiveness, coveting, and eventually rage.

But if we take the ice cube and stand on the Golden Gate Bridge and drop it into the San Francisco Bay, in an instant the ice cube disappears. The ice cube has lost its limited identity and merged into the vastness of the Pacific Ocean. But it is not simply the Pacific Ocean. The notion of a separate Pacific Ocean is an artificial distinction created by humans. In reality, the entire oceanic system that covers 70 percent of the planet is one large interconnected body of water. The one-inch cube of ice that was limited in its physical presence *is* now this entire oceanic system. It suddenly finds itself so vast and infinite that it carries within it more forms of diverse life than exist on land. It is so gigantic in its proportions that in places it is deeper than the height of Mount Everest. It is so massive in scale that gigantic tankers float on it like tiny corks. The ice cube has discovered its infinite potential, power, and capability. But it does not stop there.

The molecules of the original ice cube may evaporate off the ocean's surface and become part of a gigantic cloud. And there, as a complete miracle, a body of water that could weigh 1,000 tons floats effortlessly in the sky. The same ice cube is now floating effortlessly 10,000 feet above the earth's surface despite its staggering weight. And suddenly it could turn from a vaporous state to liquid and come down to earth as a torrential downpour and end up as water flowing in the Amazon. The same ice cube that denied it had anything to do with the river is a part of the gigantic river system and has changed its form again.

Yoga philosophy teaches us that it is similar to our human condition. We operate like the ice cube. We trap ourselves in our own sense of self-defined limitation when we could be tapping into a vastness of potential that exists inside and outside us. As Marianne Williamson wrote: "We ask ourselves, *Who am I to be brilliant, gorgeous, talented, fabulous?* Actually, who are you not to be? You are a child of God. Your playing small does not serve the world."

It is our sense of separation that leads to a distrust or dislike that we experience because the "other" outside of us has a different ethnicity, nationality, orientation, socioeconomic status, imagined privilege, religious belief, or an endless other set of attributes we can pick on. And it is that sense of separation that leads to other forms of suffering as we make comparisons with the wealth, beauty, success, possessions, and an endless set of other stories we carry in our head. Ancient wisdom traditions, travel, the interconnection made possible by the technology of the Internet—gateways such as these offer a space through which, like the ice cube, we can merge into the vastness of the river-ocean-water system of the earth and lose our sense of separation, our sense of limitation.

PART II

CLEAR OUT YOUR IN-BOX

In the New Camaldoli Hermitage on the rugged Big Coast, 11 monks support their monastery by providing retreat facilities with a killer URL: www.contemplation .com. For a group of reclusive monks they seem pretty savvy about digital marketing and early landgrab on the Internet. They're also extremely tuned in to focusing on their inner-net, leading a rich inner life dedicated to their practice based on meditation, silence, and contemplation. They've found a balance—embracing the reach of the Internet to devote themselves to principles that resonate with them deeply.

It's a challenging balance we all have to strike: engaging without losing ourselves. We log in to our mobile devices, and suddenly we're overwhelmed. *Oh, my God! I wake up in the morning and there are already 87 messages that have come to me!* So we pause, breathe, and clear out our in-box, systematically scythe through the social media message alerts, e-mails, meeting requests. We delete, organize into folders, and prioritize. We address. We hack away, making room for what matters. One message at a time.

STILLNESS IN A MADDENING BOOMTOWN

Dubai is Las Vegas with an Arabian soul. It sits shimmering on a desert. It is hot. It is booming. It is brash, bold, and breathtaking in ambition. It has an air of supreme self-confidence. Its singular purpose in life seems to be to make you gasp.

It is a maddening boomtown that is constructing 500 buildings all at once. Driving down the main artery of Sheikh Zayed Road is like driving through a sea of half-constructed buildings with giant cranes defining the skyline. The deceased ruler of Dubai, His Highness Sheikh Rashid bin Saeed Al Maktoum, had the grand vision of making Sheikh Zayed Road more spectacular than the Manhattan skyline and making this area the Wall Street of the Middle East. His subjects are making his vision come true. The construction projects underway when I visit add up to over US$220 billion. For a city with a population of four million people, that is $50,000 per person in construction projects, one of the highest per capita expenditures in the world.

But arcane numbers reminiscent of a World Bank report don't convey the scale and grandeur of this ambition. The outlandishness of the projects themselves leaves you breathless. Dubai has the world's only self-proclaimed "seven-star hotel"—the Burj Al Arab—with suites that are renting for $8,000 per night at the time of my visit. It has boldly erected the tallest building in the world—the Burj Khalifa. In the Hydropolis, a hotel fully underwater, guests stare back at peeping fish outside their windows.

The Palm Islands, off the coast, are the three largest man-made islands in the world—the self-declared "Eighth Wonder of the World." (Clearly Dubai is not shy of self-assigned superlatives.) Each of the islands is built in the shape of a date palm tree, with a trunk and a crown with fronds, all surrounded by a crescent island that acts as a breakwater. The islands support luxury hotels, freehold residential villas, unique water homes, shoreline apartments, marinas, water theme parks, restaurants, shopping malls, sports facilities, health spas, cinemas, and various diving sites. Because of their immense scale and unique shape, the islands are visible with the naked eye from outer space. With the amount of material Dubai has poured into a single Palm Island, you could build a two-meter-high wall that would circle the globe three times.

Three people I meet highlight the insanely explosive economy at a human level. Unni, who rooms with my cousin Bachu—my host in Dubai—has a job that is to make sure there are enough spare parts for the dredging machines working on the Palm Islands. My cousin Gudi's husband, Suresh, buys scrap steel from the old buildings that are being torn down and exports them to steel-smelting plants around the world. A friend of a friend, Nandu, is moving his entire family and 26 years of his life from nearby Bahrain to Dubai, hoping to make a fortune by sup-plying a single product—the flanges that will go into the steel structures of these skyscrapers. The sum total of this frenzy is an economy that is exuding confidence, brash-ness, arrogance, and an aura of invincibility.

With Bachu, I fondly reminisce about our childhood, when our harried parents would ship us all back to our home village in southern India to spend the summers with our grandparents. Our merry band of young cousins would roam the village with anarchic minds and attempt to be a threat to orderly civil society. We would spend the languid summer afternoons felling tender coconuts, eat-ing ripe mangos bursting out of their skins, and sneak-ing away to frolic in the fast-moving, rain-swollen *Puzha* (river) behind my grandparents' house that we were forbid-den to visit without adult supervision. Now Bachu and his roommates promise me a different kind of adventure—an evening I will remember, Dubai-style.

Our first stop is a desert safari in Margham. Imran, our Pakistani tour guide and driver, asks us to fasten our seat belts. Then he unleashes the four-wheel-drive all-terrain ve-hicle across the desert. He tears up the sand and reshapes the dunes. We scale sheer mountains of sand and plummet down the other side, screaming in terror and delight.

When Imran pulls up at a camel farm, I introduce my-self to the herders Ali and Razaq. They in turn introduce me to their camels, Meru, Chandini, and Sheru. The cam-els look silly and badly designed. But they are also very affectionate and nuzzle against me like lovers who need a little attention. I talk to the Urdu-speaking Pakistani herders in halting Hindi, which they can understand. Ali arrived by boat 30 years ago and lives on this farm in the middle of endless sand with no electricity and no cold water. No, that is not a typo. Hot water at near-boiling temperature is abundant, but cold water is a luxury. He has kids back home, but he can't tell me how old they are. He simply does not know how to track details like that.

Our next and last stop is a desert camp where we will eat and rest before returning to the city. Our hosts extend legendary Bedouin hospitality. We start off with deeply satisfying drags on an apple-flavored, rosewater-scented Sheesha, followed by a feast of pita bread, hummus, lamb, chicken, beef kabobs, dates, and Arab coffee. Suddenly the music changes to a Middle Eastern wail with a pulsing beat. As we recline on intricate rugs and comfortable beds in the middle of the desert, two Tunisian belly dancers glide into the center and weave a mesmerizing magic. I feel like an Arabian prince.

When the party is finally over, our hosts ask us to look at the star-filled sky and listen to the quiet sounds of a desert night. They say the stillness has not changed in a thousand years. The thought strikes me: just a few hours ago and a few miles away, I was surrounded by the noise and lights and chaos of a city intent on catapulting itself into the future. Now, under the desert stars, I feel I am returning to something ancient, wild, and sacred—reconnecting with something essential to my soul. We need these oases of wildness in all our modern places—that's why in the middle of New York City you need Central Park. In Dubai, the contrast is simply starker as the brand-new and the timeless collide.

It strikes me then why Thoreau left Boston to live near Walden Pond. Why sage philosophers in India have long retreated into the stillness of the Himalayas. Why designer Philippe Starck stays on the cutting edge by living, as he said, "alone mostly, in the middle of nowhere." Why

Manhattan investment bankers flock to the Berkshires and Hamptons during the weekend. And why Saudi billionaire investor Prince Al-Waleed bin Talal routinely retires to desert camps and sits in the starlit stillness (in gilded tents and with a retinue of servants, of course). A memory that is etched into my mind is that soon after Prince Al Waleed took a big investment position at Citibank, then chairman and CEO John Reed joined him on a desert retreat, reclining on fabulous carpets, leaning against a bolster, under the desert sky, and wearing an abaya.

It does not matter who we are, how urban our life is, or how plugged in we are to the rhythms of modern life. Much like birth and death, some rhythms of our life have not changed for a thousand years and will not change for the next thousand. Even as Dubai hurtles into the future, the people there deeply understand the wisdom that they learned from their Bedouin forefathers: that in the stillness of nature, deep in the womb of the desert, is where they find their recharging station. That is where the chattering mind pauses and shifts into a different phase of consciousness. That is where we find space to identify and put aside what is not essential. And that is where, like Philippe Starck or Bill Gates during his much-written-about "think weeks," we reconnect with our creative soul. Find your desert safari, find your Margham. Go. Often.

Do One Thing at a Time

Last week I was standing at the Chicago airport and noticed a young woman in front of me in the security line. She looked as though she was traveling on business, perhaps returning home after a meeting. She was eating her lunch sandwich while at the same time typing something on her iPad. And as the line inched forward she kept her place, pushing her bag forward with her feet.

Suddenly her cell phone rang. She answered the phone and cradled it between her shoulder and neck, still holding her sandwich in one hand and doing one-finger typing on her iPad with the other hand and propelling her bag forward with her legs. By now she had reached the desk where the officer was checking identification and boarding pass. She placed her iPad on the counter and retrieved her driver's license from her handbag, all the while still cradling the phone between her shoulder and neck and continuing the conversation. She was now doing five things simultaneously. And I thought to myself, *How did we reach here as a civilization? How did we survive as a species?*

The one thing I have learned to do over the years, using trial and error and some hard knocks, is to practice doing one thing at a time. It sounds simple—almost pedestrian. It's on the same level as someone saying that if you eat vegetables and exercise regularly, you will feel better. But underneath this very simplistic-sounding wisdom there is a profound secret that people from heart surgeons to professional athletes to world-class musicians have discovered, adopted, and mastered.

In today's hyperconnected, fast-charging lifestyles, there is a tendency to do too much at the same time and get very distracted in the process—a tendency that blogger Linda Stone has called *continuous partial attention*. "To be busy and connected is to feel alive," Stone writes. "But the consequence is that we're over-stimulated, over-wound, unfulfilled." Our productivity suffers too. At work, for example, I have caught myself in meetings being tempted to check and respond to e-mail even as one of my colleagues is presenting something. And simultaneously I'm likely to have a few chat windows open in parallel conversations and be trying to inhale my lunch as well.

I'm getting everything done at once, or so it seems. However, when I look back I see that my time was actually not that productive. I'm not really sure of anything I "got done." I can't recall any details of what was presented. I can't remember the flavors of my food or even tell you what I ate. Except that there is food spilled on my keyboard that gives me some clues. And I have sent an embarrassing message in the wrong chat window.

This technology that is our brain is exceptionally good at focusing on one thing at a time—not more. There must be a reason why you never see an accomplished violinist practicing the violin while watching a game on television. Our brain also takes time to switch from one task to another, and the incessant back-and-forth required by doing too many things at once drains our energy. The brain takes time to exit one task and gather itself around the next task. Whichever Zen master told us, "Eat when hungry, sleep when tired" had something profound on his mind beyond just a witty one-liner.

What works for me is a simple system. I pick the most important and urgent single task in front of me. I set a timer and power through the single task in a focused manner. When I am done or the timer goes off, I stop—or work a few extra minutes until I reach a stopping point—then take a short break of a few minutes, get some water, or take a short walk on the floor or outdoors. Then I tackle the next most important single task.

Sometimes, if I need to work on a large task, such as drafting a presentation I'm giving at a meeting in Toronto, I'll alternate tasks. I might work on my presentation for 30 minutes, attend to e-mails for another 30, and then switch back to my presentation. In contrast, if I'm working toward a tight deadline, then I might stay with that task until I'm finished. The system allows for flexibility; the choice is yours.

The second thing I do is make appointments with myself. I block out chunks of time in my calendar that read, for example, "Work block to finish customer presentation." So instead of responding to e-mails as they come, I will block out two hours just for e-mail and process hundreds of messages in one sitting. When it is a formal appointment—even though it's with myself—I am more likely to commit myself to doing that task. And if you are in a corporate setting, no one else is going to spot an open window on your calendar that they can hijack to draw your attention to something else.

According to Tony Schwartz, who wrote in a *Harvard Business Review* blog in 2013 about the cost of multitasking,

"The biggest cost is to your productivity. In part, that's a simple consequence of splitting your attention, so that you're partially engaged in multiple activities but rarely fully engaged in any one. In part, it's because when you switch away from a primary task to do something else, you're increasing the time it takes to finish that task by an average of 25 percent. But most insidiously, it's because if you're always doing something, you're relentlessly burning down your available reservoir of energy over the course of every day, so you have less available with every passing hour."

A simple suggestion that Tony makes is to do the most important thing first in the morning, for 60 to 90 minutes, with a clear start and stop time. Resist every impulse to distraction, knowing that you have a designated stopping point. The more absorbed you can get, the more productive you'll be. When you're done, take a few minutes to recharge. "When you're engaged at work, fully engage, for defined periods of time," he writes. "When you're renewing, truly renew. . . . Stop living your life in the gray zone."

I tried hard for years to be the first person in the history of humankind to prove that multitasking really works—that we can be effective in the "gray zone." Paradoxically, I have found that doing one thing at a time actually helps me get more things done and do them better. Here is the dirty little secret. Our brain is one of the most complex, sophisticated working systems we know of. Give it one task to focus on and it can perform brilliantly. Give it five tasks to do at once and it crumbles. Why mess with it?

Gathering
at the River

It is of biblical, or more appropriately Vedic, proportions. Somewhere between 50 and 70 million attendees have squeezed through this tiny Himalayan foothill town on the banks of the river Ganga (Ganges), where a dip during the festival ensures the faithful a cleansing of sins and a shortcut to Nirvana. I am at the Maha Kumbh Mela in Haridwar, India: the largest gathering and festival (*mela*) of humanity on earth and a staggering act of faith.

The Kumbh Mela is very improbable as festivals go. There is no fixed date. It all depends on how the sun, the moon, and Jupiter align. It does not happen in one place, but cycles between Haridwar on the banks of the Ganga, Nasik on the banks of the Shipra River, Ujjain on the banks of the Godavari River, and Prayag Allahabad at the confluence of the rivers Ganga and Yamuna and the mythical Saraswati, believed to flow underground.

You have to wait for the festival to come around. The Kumbh Mela (basic) happens every 3 years, the Ardha (half) Kumbh Mela happens once every 6 years, the Purna (full) Kumbh Mela happens once in 12 years. The Maha (Big) Kumbh Mela, the mother of all Kumbh Melas, happens once in 12 times 12, or once in 144 years. The last one was in 2001. So your great-grandchildren's great-grandchildren will get to see it next in 2145. The astrologers have already determined the best dates for that Kumbh. How is that for long-range planning? And they have been figuring this out since A.D. 600, as far as we know, long before they could use computers to do the math.

In any case, the Kumbh Mela has been happening for a long, long time. It traces its roots back to a time when the Devatas (gods) and the Asuras (demons) decided to be friends for a while and churn the great oceans to get to the Amrita—the sweet elixir of immortality—at the bottom. After 30 years of churning, out came the Kumbh (pitcher) with the elixir in it—but predictably the deities started squabbling. Indra, the king of the gods, directed his son Jayanta to secure the pitcher. Jayanta did a good job hanging on to it, although he was hotly pursued around the universe by the Asuras for 12 years. Fortunately for us, Jayanta spilled a few drops on the earth into those four rivers—Ganga, Shipra, Godavari, and Yamuna—giving mere mortals a chance to attain immortality.

The real miracle of the Kumbh Mela is that there is no promotional campaign announcing it. There is no central organization running it. The dates get published in the Hindu almanac. Word gets around. The faithful start converging. And this being India, when the population stirs, it means a million people show up. There are masses of Hindus who arrive from the cities, towns, and villages on buses, trains, planes, boat, and camels, as well as on foot. The stars of the show are the Hindu holy men—sadhus, Babas, gurus, ascetics, yogis, and mystics—who converge from their ashrams on the plains and their caves in the Himalayas. Predictably there are the *National Geographic* photographers, the BBC camera crew, the inveterate

Lonely Planet travelers, and gawkers like me. A part-time French sadhu rode his bike all the way here. And on an impulse I told my boss at Google, "I am running away to India for a few days," then caught a plane in San Francisco to fly halfway around the world and arrive by train, road, boat, and finally on foot to experience the magic for myself.

My companion for the trip is Manpreet Vohra, an Indian diplomat. He has always said yes to my mad adventures. And so it is that we have climbed Mount Kilimanjaro in Tanzania, explored Genghis Khan's capital Karakorum in the Gobi desert, watched lions prey on hapless wildebeest in the Serengeti, and talked to Malayalee fishermen as they hauled in their catch on the Malabar Coast in India. Now, before we hit the bustling anarchy of the festival, we want to experience the serenity and purity of the Ganges River in its upper reaches where the snowmelt swooshes down from Gangotri, straight from Lord Shiva's hair, as legend has it. We raft down the whitewater from Shivpuri to Rishikesh, the world capital of ashrams and yogis. As we glide down the rapids, we pass sadhus at the water's edge doing their daily rituals and worshiping the river. A sport that is three decades old in India comes face-to-face with a tradition of three millennia.

The epicenter of the Kumbh Mela is a bathing ghat called Har Ki Pauri. This is where Jayanta dropped some elixir into the Bhrama Kund, so it is the best place to take a dip. As the sun goes down, huge crowds gather to offer Arati, fire worship, to the river. I am one of 21 designated people waving the big Arati lamps tonight. A Hindu priest helps me hold a five-level oil lamp with more than 100 individual flames and swing it in wide circles. The atmosphere is electric as 50,000 voices sing in unison, "Jai

Gange Arati . . ." The river glistens and glides swiftly in its onward journey to the Bay of Bengal as it has been doing for a million years. The smells, sounds, and colors all assault the senses. It is one of the most moving acts of faith I have ever experienced.

The main attractions at any Kumbh Mela are the sadhus—the mystics and Hindu holy men. On designated days they march in a procession to the river ordered by some complex rules I don't fully grasp. The superstars among them are the Naga Babas, and ironically they are also the hardest to find. Even among a community of people who have set aside conventional life, the Naga Babas are on the extreme edge as fierce ascetics. They have renounced almost everything we can imagine. They are capable of living in serene detachment and contentment under a tree, as I saw some of them doing, or in a luxurious palace, should they be invited to stay for a few days as some of them are by their followers. But they remain aloof from it all, always.

Late one night, I come upon a group of Naga Babas camped out around their ceremonial fire pits. Several of them are sitting in a circle talking to two international visitors. The group looks welcoming, so I walk toward the circle and offer my greeting: "Om Namasivaya." "Om Namasivaya," the group echoes, and asks me to join them. Phiri Giri Baba, a senior Naga Baba, is in conversation with a German man and a Yugoslavian woman, both visiting the Kumbh Mela. He tells us his life story, how he entered this life when he was a teenager, the challenges of the path, what it takes to become a Naga Baba, the joy and freedom with which he lives. And then just like that, he predicts that at the next Kumbh Mela he will take

Samadhi, when he will exit his body and leave his mortal coil behind.

When I say good-bye to my new friend Maharaj Phiri Giri Baba, sitting on the banks of the river, he sucks deeply on his hash pipe and asks for my address. I find a business card, thinking it will be the simplest way to respond. He looks at my card briefly and says something that makes me jump with surprise and delight as a Google marketing person. Here is someone who has never used a computer, does not speak much English, dropped out of eighth grade to pursue an ascetic lifestyle. He looks at my card and says in Hindi, "Oh, yes, Google, very powerful website."

One early morning as I walk the banks of the Ganges I see another Naga Baba with his dreadlocked hair coiled on top, his body covered with ash, pacing at the water's edge. He is not deep in meditation. He is not chanting Sanskrit mantras. He is not in an advanced yoga pose. Instead he is speaking excitedly on a mobile phone, jabbing his finger in the air. Perhaps he is talking to his stockbroker about mobile phone stocks—or to the god Shiva himself. It is an interesting sight. The one thing that this Naga Baba has yet to renounce is his cell phone!

I leave the Kumbh Mela thinking about the enormity of its scale, the power of its mythology, the incredible act of faith that has led millions to gather at the river for more than 1,400 years. Today, many of us gather by the river called Internet, where data flows even swifter than water, and information is oxygen. But as I think about the swami with the cell phone, and the Baba who knows Google, it occurs to me that this may not be as different as it seems.

In my multiple visits to India, this is something that has stood out in my mind: how the ancient and modern don't simply collide, but meld and coexist. The computer scientist who will put a marigold garland and a red tilak on his workstation during Saraswati Puja in honor of Saraswati, the goddess of learning, to bless the tools of his trade just like his great-grandfather did with his plough or hammer. Silicon Valley entrepreneurs of Indian origin getting the priest from the Hindu temple to do Bhoomi Puja for the new data center and gifting him stock options. Perhaps this explains why India has survived as a civilization for 5,000 years and outlasted many invasions: it has this unique ability to be firmly rooted in its past. It has a rock to stand on while stepping forward with the other foot, testing the quicksand of an uncertain but exciting future.

FIND MEANING AND PURPOSE

I've been traveling on the train from Tiruchchirappalli for more than six hours. It's dark now, and I'm almost to my destination—Chennai, a teeming city of four million people, the only place I know in all of southern India where I can access a copy of *U.S. News and World Report Guide to Best Graduate Schools*. I should be at my college, the National Institute of Technology, working on my paper for my digital signal processing class or studying for the Very Large Scale Integration (of electronic circuits) exam, but I really have to be on this train, traveling to Chennai, to research graduate schools. This train journey is the first of many steps in a process ritualized over the years by fellow students who wish to attend graduate school in the United States. The students have even published the process in a guidebook—ROTGAD, or Realization of the Great American Dream.

It's 95 degrees outside, probably hotter in the train car, and there's no air-conditioning. For nearly the entire trip—seven hours and 13 stops—I've been gazing out the window as we pass towns with lyrical names like Lalgudi, Ariyalur, Tindivanam, and Chengalpattu, as we push past small villages strung along the tracks, where shadowy figures of men, women, and children move slowly beside the train.

As we approach the station in Chennai, the train screeches toward a halt. I can feel metal banging into metal as the coaches telescope into each other, hear the buffer and chain couplers screaming as they absorb the shock of the slowing train. A big jerk, a thud, and we stop. For a moment, the night is silent, then the baritone chorus of a dozen male voices—"Chaaai, Chaaai, Chaaai"—as the masala tea wallahs walk by the train in the dim station light, offering their steaming hot tea.

Unlike the train, the U.S. Information Services library offers me a level of comfort and elegance. Air-conditioned, orderly, and hushed silence. Feeling a little important, accomplished, I take the copy of the guidebook to an empty table, sit, and write down the schools that interest me on a piece of paper. I avoid the big names that intimidate me—Harvard, MIT, Stanford. I eye schools like Louisiana State, the University of Florida, and the Oregon Graduate Center.

At 9 P.M. I check into a youth hostel to spend the night in the only place I can afford. There are 20 beds, many of them taken by students like me or young men from Jaffna in Sri Lanka, fleeing the conflict there and waiting for a visa to another country on a refugee status. The next day, on the way back to the college campus, I'm exhausted and thrilled by the possibilities of the information I now hold securely in my hands.

I spent more than 24 hours to retrieve that information. Fourteen hours on the train alone. Today, with the Internet, I could have located the list of schools in ten seconds. Then, I had access to information, but that information trickled in slowly.

My grandparents working their rice farm in their rural Indian village were almost completely cut off from the outside world. And though my parents had a bit more access in the village government schools they attended for ten years, it was limited as well. When I was growing up in the small towns my father's job took us to—before computer-assisted learning programs, and years before the Internet took off in the way we know it today—we had greater access. In each town, hungry to learn, we soaked up information through our studies, our friends, outside reading, the news—all we were exposed to. A bit of information would propel us forward. From that point we'd learn more, and shoot forward again, or sideways—all different directions. In high school, I read in one of the local papers that by the year 2000 there would be a huge demand for engineers in the electronics and computer science industries. As a result of that information, those industries were on my radar, and I gravitated toward those studies. Despite my parents' extremely modest education, my three siblings and I have ten college degrees among us, including two degrees from Ivy League business schools. How did we manage such a leap? Access to information.

After my research that day in the library, I applied to ten U.S. graduate programs. All accepted me but none offered scholarships, which I needed, so I went to the Indian Institute of Management, an excellent program in India. Years later, when I was working in New York, I saw an ad for the Wharton MBA program at the University of Pennsylvania. I went to an informational meeting, applied to the school, and made the wait list. The second year I was accepted.

During my first week at Wharton, alumnus David Pottruck, then CEO of Charles Schwab, spoke to us about purpose. We were enormously blessed, he said, and should be grateful that after graduating, one of our biggest struggles would be choosing from the many fantastic job offers we would receive. His one piece of advice? Pick the job that would give us the greatest sense of meaning and purpose, the values and activities that resonated deeply within us and served ourselves and others in some way. He said that during his early career he was in a job that didn't resonate with him. When he looked for a new one, his search uncovered several potential jobs. The one that appealed to him most paid the least and was the least glamorous, but that job with a financial firm in New York City was the one that aligned with his meaning and purpose, so that's the job he chose. He spent his first months working in a basement office, working at a desk that rattled like crazy whenever the J train passed by underground.

David Pottruck loved that job. He put all his being, his heart and soul into that job. He excelled, and his performance accelerated his career. As further opportunities presented themselves, David continued to choose those in which he found meaning and purpose, and he advanced rapidly. David's words have stayed with me.

I define my own purpose as living to my highest potential and helping others achieve the same. Peace, freedom, and happiness are my highest values. When I've considered job opportunities, I've always asked myself, *Which holds the most meaning for me? Which aligns most closely with my purpose?* And I've gravitated toward that option. I ask myself the same question when choosing which projects to sign up for at work. That technique has served me well in all aspects of my life, including my decision to work at Google.

One of the things I love most about Google is that I'm helping people get their hands on information they could not normally access. For example, with Google Maps Street View, you can "walk down" any street on the planet. You can even visit shops, restaurants, and architectural wonders. You can step through the doors of the white marble Taj Mahal in Agra, India. In Google Ocean, you can follow deep-sea divers as they navigate oceans around the globe. That information can open worlds.

Imagine this scenario: Children in a school in Okhaldhunga, Nepal, living high in the mountains of a landlocked country, with no ocean anywhere near. They have never even seen the ocean. But now, with access to the Internet, they can sit at their computers or pick up their phones, and go into Google Ocean. Picture them sitting around, clicking away, taking in the ocean—from the air, on the beach, or underwater, exploring marine life in the Galápagos Islands, the Barrier Reef, Molokini Crater in Hawai'i. Kids looking at forms of life they have never seen before, that they didn't even know existed. Think of the learning this information ignites, the opportunities it creates, the lives this information can truly change. That is the kind of thing that we are doing at Google.

When Sergey Brin and Larry Page founded Google, they captured their purpose in a simple sentence: "Google's mission is to organize the world's information and make it universally accessible and useful." In more than 17 years, Sergey, Larry, and the employees at Google have aligned with that purpose, creating amazing outcomes and great opportunities, not just for themselves but for billions of people on the planet.

Periodically, I go back to Chittilamchery to visit relatives. We go as a family—my parents, my siblings, their spouses, their kids. When we're there, my parents often want to participate in ceremonies held in the village temple, so we all go. Sometimes we drive by the school where my mother studied. It hasn't changed much in terms of physical infrastructure, but what *has* changed in that school, and in tens of thousands of other schools around the world, is that the kids in these schools now have access to the Internet, including the services we build at Google. Those kids can access the same information as any student at Stanford or Harvard can.

Google is just one tiny player in the vast ecosystem of technical innovation. In this day and age, where information powers the world and makes us all smarter, we're all providing access to information, inspiring others, leveling the playing field for humanity, and that is what gives me a great sense of meaning and purpose in my work; that is what I want to pour my energy into. That is why I do the work I do.

One of my good friends is Chade-Meng Tan, a pioneering engineer at Google, a creator of Google University's Search Inside Yourself program, and self-appointed "Jolly Good Fellow." Meng lives by his personal mission statement, one of the clearest, shortest, most direct, and most powerful mission statements I've ever heard: "To create conditions for world peace in my lifetime." As one of the original employees at Google, number 107, Meng attained huge financial success. After eight years at Google, he found he had many options before him. He could continue to build Google technologies, or he could do something else entirely with his wealth.

Meng chose to build his life around his mission statement, so he stayed at Google, changed his title and career path, and set out to study more, listen more, and read the works of His Holiness the Dalai Lama. One thing the Dalai Lama wrote stuck with him: "We can never obtain peace in the outer world until we find peace within ourselves." Meng knows that the way to achieve inner peace is through contemplative practices, so, working with experts in the use of mindfulness at work, he developed a class to teach mindfulness-based emotional intelligence to employees at Google. Because Google is a highly scientific, research-oriented environment, which draws like-minded people, Meng worked with Stanford University and other researchers to scientifically prove the effectiveness of his class.

His program, Search Inside Yourself (SIY), became the most popular training program at Google, with a huge waiting list. The demand for the course, the hunger for the knowledge it offers, has been amazing and intriguing. Hundreds and hundreds of technology people line up not to learn about the next artificial intelligence programming techniques or machine language methodologies but to begin the journey to inner peace.

Meng went on to publish the *New York Times* bestseller *Search Inside Yourself,* which is being translated into dozens of languages. He speaks around the world about mindfulness, and has founded the Search Inside Yourself Leadership Institute, or SIYLI (pronounced "silly"), in honor of his personal motto, "Life is too important to be taken seriously." He hopes the international training program will eventually contribute to world peace in a meaningful way. All this—the course, the program, the research, the book, spreading the word—evolved from Meng honoring his core purpose, to create conditions for world peace in his lifetime.

Perhaps you're thinking this sounds rather lofty. But your core purpose doesn't have to involve world peace. You may find meaning and purpose in moving mortgages or assets or dedicating yourself to your new baby, which holds more meaning for you than anything in the world.

What do I mean by "meaning" and "purpose"? We're each blessed with unique talents and gifts. These talents might be music or sculpting or engineering. Maybe you have a gift for coaxing vegetables and flowers from seeds, or organizing and orchestrating flavors and textures to create an amazing meal for your family. You might have the ability to make people feel good about themselves, or you're a natural caregiver, or you're great with kids and teach kindergarten. It doesn't matter. Everyone is uniquely blessed.

How do we determine our gifts? If each one of us looks back on our life, we can always point to a time when we completely lost our sense of self, lost our sense of time, when we engaged with what we were doing in an almost selfless and joyous way. Maybe it was poring over data to analyze the cause of the slowdown in shipments; or organizing a fund-raiser for Team in Training, the Leukemia & Lymphoma Society's endurance sports training program; or building a model remote-control glider and watching it soar. Those times provide clues about what we find deeply meaningful and where our talents and gifts lie. When we use these gifts to express ourselves, our heart sings, we're in the zone. These gifts are meaningful to us.

Then you might go a step further and ask yourself, *Does doing what holds meaning for me serve a purpose?* Is cooking or analyzing data or teaching something that serves me, serves someone in my life, or serves the world at large in a positive way?

When you determine your purpose, you can start aligning with it, to make sure how you spend your time and focus your energy holds meaning for you and serves that purpose. On a daily basis, can you go to bed at night and say to yourself, *I am happy I chose to spend those three hours on a particular activity?* The idea is to consciously ask yourself questions, consciously make the choice, consciously direct your life toward what resonates deeply within you and brings you joy.

FOCUS ON THE ESSENTIAL

Fourteen years ago, in the middle of the dot-com boom, I joined the founding management team of a Silicon Valley start-up. Working for a start-up is unbelievably stressful, and leading one is even more so. At our start-up, each day brought a myriad of challenges—the server kept crashing, the biggest deal we'd signed was about to unravel, our top networking engineer had decided to jump to a more well-funded competitor, and if we didn't raise our next round of funding, we wouldn't make payroll.

Finally, in the midst of the chaos, I called a friend who needed a break as much as I did, and, bags packed, we headed for Lucia on the Big Sur coast to go on a retreat with 11 Camaldolese monks in the New Camaldoli Hermitage. These monks are extremely tuned in to their inner-net, and they encourage their guests to observe the same focus on meditation, silence, and contemplation.

The retreat is in the mountains, overlooking the Pacific Ocean, on the craggiest part of the coastline. My friend Suku and I had separate rooms, the idea being that if you shared, you'd be tempted to just chitchat away— definitely against policy, and especially true of someone like me. I would have kept Suku awake all night. He and

I are voracious readers and avid explorers. He's been to 83 countries, and I've been to 54. We can and do talk endlessly about anything and everything from geopolitics to tribes in Papua New Guinea. From stories about life in our college dorm, fluctuations in the Baltic shipping index because of the Chinese buying all container capacity, and Komodo dragons to biologist E. O. Wilson's obsession with studying ants. On this trip, though, we explored the hermitage, and we read, but we rarely spoke.

We spent our time in our rooms or just outside our rooms in our private gardens—wild sage, scrub grass, palms, olive trees—overlooking the ocean below. I spent hours there, soaking up the sun, staring out to sea, trying to calm my tightly wound nerves. Twice a day, the monks prepared meals and laid them out in the dining room, for us to take back to our rooms. In silence. It was a beautiful, beautiful experience.

If guests wanted to speak, we had to walk down the hill and off the property. Otherwise, we were encouraged to take our time to reflect in silence with nature and with ourselves. And yet, at first, instead of contemplating nature, I found myself contemplating the start-up. I kept coming back to our business plan—growth, differentiators, execution—the last thing I wanted to focus on. But there it was. Finally, instead of fighting my wayward mind, I just sat with my thoughts. Back to the business plan. A solid business plan was essential for our company to operate and for the employees to align with a common goal, to work as a team to get their work done. Most important, venture capitalists wouldn't look twice unless we had a strong, focused business plan. We *did* have a solid plan that aligned with our mission, our meaning and purpose as a company. And that got me thinking about creating a business plan for my life.

For the past few years, since I'd heard David Pottruck speak at Wharton about the importance of aligning career choices with our meaning and purpose, I'd lived with that idea in mind, but I had not developed a specific plan. I had not determined essential principles to support my meaning and purpose. So at the hermitage, I sat in my garden, contemplating what those essentials might be. After a few minutes, I opened my eyes, picked up a pencil, and started writing down the organizing principles of my life.

I wanted to stick to one page. Simply, I wanted to be able to pick up that one piece of paper and say, "These are the organizing principles of my life." When I'd filled my page, I decided I wanted more clarity. Could I distill my organizing principles into five words? I did. Five words. At any time, I could look at my essentials, tattooed, metaphorically, on my fingertips, and say, "These are the things that are most important in my life. These are my essentials. These give me meaning and purpose."

For example, one of my essentials is health, which encompasses all aspects of health—spiritual, emotional, physical, mental, and financial. So I focus my time and energy on activities that support health and try to avoid activities that don't. Saying yes to the essential allows you to say no to a lot of other things that are nonessential. I won't go into the rest of my five essentials. It doesn't matter what they are. Your essentials will be your own.

I will say that I now spend 80 percent of my life energy on those five essentials. The rest, about 20 percent, I treat as a distraction, an obligation—a meeting I have to go to or a dinner party I have to attend that might take away from the time and energy I could spend on focusing on meditation, or yoga, or even running the half marathons I take part in once a year with the simple goal of seeing if I'm physically fit enough to reach the finish line alive. I look at the distractions that take up 20 percent of my time as the tax I have to pay on what is a fabulous life. Focusing on my five essentials has changed the quality of my life, what I choose to do with my time, and the joy that manifests as a result.

Some find it hard to get started, to find the time to devote to creating a list. You don't have to create your list all in one sitting. Some may find it hard to find anything that brings them joy at the moment. You can start to create your list by jotting down something that brings even the smallest lift at this point in your life. Or you may start out with a huge list—maybe 200 items. Then you can begin scything through the list, asking yourself, "What are things that are really not all that important?" Throw out items you spend time on that aren't serving you well. Keep returning to your list over a period of time until you have a handful of essentials, preferably a single-digit number, fewer than ten, ideally fewer than five. Those are your top priorities and everything else is noise.

Susan Wojcicki, the CEO of YouTube, owned by Google, follows what she calls her Three Big Rocks method. Susan, employee number 16, has been with Google from the beginning. In 1998, when she was pregnant and worried about making her mortgage payment, Susan rented her garage on Santa Margarita Avenue in Menlo Park to Larry Page and Sergey Brin, who set up shop and founded Google in that small space, only six miles from the current headquarters. Susan has a phenomenal track record both at Google and in the business world. In 2015, she was included in *Time* magazine's list of the 100 Most Influential People. Not only is she a senior executive, she's also the mother of five, dedicated to her kids, available to help with homework and organize birthday parties—she's there for them.

I've known Susan for years. One day I pulled her aside. "At any point in time," I said, "you have sixty-two things calling out for your attention, a hundred things to worry about. How do you keep it all in your head? How do you stay sane through it all?" She told me she cuts through the chaos and chatter, and zeros in on the three essential elements that will ensure radical progress forward, that will determine success for the piece of business that she is managing at that time. Susan's in Silicon Valley, working for Google at YouTube, so she relies on an extremely high-tech system to track her three essentials. She writes three items on a Post-it note, and sticks the Post-it to her computer monitor.

When I returned from the retreat in Big Sur, I took a hard look at where I was spending my time to see if I was distributing the hours in my day somewhat evenly across my essentials. Clearly I was not. At work, I was so keenly focused on driving the business forward that I'd lost sight of any of the essentials I wanted to bring to my business in the first place. And outside of work? There was no outside of work. I had some balancing to do, and I began right away—incorporating my essentials into my work life and my home life, creating balance.

You don't have to sequester yourself in a monastery to create your list of essentials. Your car, your office, or your kitchen table late at night will work just as well. Just so it's quiet, someplace peaceful, where you can find spaciousness within yourself. Sit down and ask yourself, *What are my essentials?* Be clear about what is most important to you. The process doesn't have to be overly complicated. Your list can be very simple, whatever comes immediately to mind. Your family, for example, your health, your financial success. It doesn't matter. Just get crystal clear, and narrow your list to a few objectives. Then, when chaos reigns, bring your attention back to what's essential to you. When you're feeling confused, focus on the essential. When your focus wanders, bring it back to what matters most. Just bring it back.

TEN THINGS TO
DO WITH THE
NEXT HOUR

No matter who it is making it, I always hear the same lament. CEOs of companies tell me they are overworked. Farmers back in my home village in southern India, they say they have no time. We can all complain that we are under the tyranny of schedules, that there is no time in our day. Each of us can say that much of our life is driven by someone else's agenda or outside pressures—things we have to do, things we would like to do, things we are expected to do.

When I graduated from business school and went to work at McKinsey & Company, I had a terrible time organizing my day. Seven days a week, work was my number-one priority. I fed on the thrill of accomplishments. I dashed to meetings, raced to meet flights, ate whatever food was given to me—airline food and conference food, which is terrible stuff. My house was a mess—stacks of bills that I was too busy to open, let alone pay, suitcases half unpacked from the last trip and partially packed for the next. A few times my phone was cut off or my credit card declined. Not because I didn't have the money, but because I was trying to focus so much on my work and travel that I didn't have the time to pay bills. It was embarrassing, as though I couldn't take control of my own life. This chaos went on for quite a long time—almost a year—until I reached my breaking point, and started asking myself, *Why am I living this life? What is the purpose of it? What am I trying to do here? And what is the price I am paying?* My life had become travel, bad food, and not enough exercise and meditation. And I realized that I had to reprioritize.

A few years ago, I was in New York, attending several programs led by one of my spiritual teachers, Mata Amritanandamayi, or Amma (mother), as she's more commonly known. As I sat in meditation, my mind wandered, and I started thinking about how we each have only 24 hours in our day, and how so much of the quality of our lives, the quality of our joy, the quality of our presence—how we feel, what we do, what we accomplish— is predicated on how we choose to spend those 24 hours. I asked myself, *If I only had a few hours—or just one hour— fully under my control, what would be the next one thing I would choose to do with it that would maximize this quality of joy, presence, and life? What would support my five essentials on a day-to-day basis?* I came up with ten items. As the list developed, the idea switched from a theoretical notion to a tactical way to structure my days that would support what's important to me in my life, what resonates and brings me joy.

The items in my list are global, but within those larger categories, I focus on specific activities that work for me. For example, if I want to spend time on "growth," my number nine, I might pull out the harmonium and practice the song that I learned in India on this trip, which would also support number eight, "passions," because music is a passion of mine.

Your list of how to spend your hours in each day might contain different items with different priorities. My list has changed my life, and I'd like to share it with you.

1. **Sleep:** If I had a few hours to spend as I wished, then the first choice I would make would be to spend those hours sleeping. Ideally for eight hours. Sleeping dictates how we feel physically and emotionally, which affects our level of joy. We violate that simple rule and the laws of nature can respond with ruthless brutality. I remember being at work one day and receiving a desperate ping from my good friend Sarah, a hardware engineer who also studied dance in college. Sarah has a particular passion for going out swing dancing on weeknights that keeps her up late when she should be in bed. "Gopi," she confessed, "I am not processing information very well at work today."

2. **Nutrition:** We all know that what we put into our bodies can support or sabotage our well-being, our state of happiness, our joy, our energy, our health, how well we think, and our creativity. Conscious nutrition means we're mindful of what we put between our lips. I'd love to say I'm 100 percent conscious all the time, but I'm not. I recall attending an official business dinner in my first job after college, and getting carried away with my business colleagues, bingeing on the free food and alcohol, and staying up late. Spicy

Madrasi, Old Monk rum and Coke, and aloo parataha—talk about sabotage. I'll never forget the embarrassment of nodding off the next day in a meeting with my boss and a senior executive of Indian Railways. Whether we grow our own food, cook our own food, or even just eat food made by somebody else—it's important to choose and eat our food consciously and mindfully. So if I had just another 30 minutes to play with, I would shop mindfully and choose my meals with care.

3. **Exercise:** If I had another hour, or even less, I would pick exercise as my next-highest priority. Exercise fuels my physical and mental energy. Often when I'm traveling, I can't fit in the full hour, so I might practice a bit of yoga, maybe three or four sun salutations on a towel in my hotel room, or squeeze in 30 laps in the small hotel pool. This method works for me. You might prefer another method. Whatever you do—swim, walk, run in the hills, practice yoga, dance, or play tennis—I think it's essential to find a form of movement that delights you.

4. **Meditation:** If I found another 20 minutes available, what would I choose? Meditation. My meditation practice guides me personally and sets the tone for the rest of the day. It fills me with joy and allows me to clear my head of noise and clutter, bringing a level of clarity to my mental processes that allows me to operate at peak performance. Often I have to get creative about my meditation, and I can't always meditate before I begin my day. For example, since my job requires so much travel, I find time to meditate

on the plane during those 15 minutes during takeoff, when all electronics are turned off, there is no service, and it's very quiet.

5. **Love:** The next thing I added to my list was love—the thoughts and actions that generate love inside me, and giving time to those I love. Many might ask, "Shouldn't love be number one on the list?" I've put it fifth, because if I've not slept well, eaten well, exercised, and then found time for a little bit of mindful meditation, I can't be present and in a state of high energy and joy with myself or my loved ones. I can't operate at an optimal and peak state of love. My philosophy is no different from that of the airlines. Think about what all flight attendants tell you before takeoff: "Put on your oxygen mask first before helping someone else."

6. **Stuff:** What is the one thing I would choose to focus on with my next chunk of time? Taking care of the stuff in my life. When I say "stuff," I mean mail, dishes, and day-to-day chores that I need to take care of to keep my life running smoothly. These tasks aren't urgent or life shattering, but if I let all of them pile up, they start interfering with how I feel and how I perform.

7. **Work:** The next item that made my simple list is work. Now, don't tell my employer that my work ranks seventh. Many would put work at the top of the list, but I feel that if I take care of numbers one through six, I'm a much better performer, I deliver a higher quality of work in less time, and I find my work much more fulfilling. Give it a try.

I think you'll find that everyone benefits. You benefit, your company benefits, your co-workers benefit, and your boss should be super happy.

8. **Passions:** If I had another hour left, the one thing I would do is focus on my passions. There are things that move me, things I do because I love them, not because I have to do them or I am going to make a living out of them (although my work is also one of my passions). I have many passions—public speaking, for example, teaching yoga, singing kirtan music. So if there is an hour left in my calendar, then I put it into my passions.

9. **Growth:** Whether it's playing the harmonium, producing a TV show, cooking vegetarian food, or open-water swimming, learning helps me realize new possibilities and expand my universe.

10. **Community:** If I were lucky enough to have any time left, I would spend that time in acts of service to my community, acts that draw my energy outward. For me, that time might be teaching my yoga class at Google, simply hosting my friends for a cup of tea or dinner at home, or organizing an art project for the Burning Man community. You might work with your church or volunteer at your kids' school or help out at a shelter. Or maybe you devote your time to an act that's less structured, such as taking the time to reach out and call a friend you have not spoken with in a long while or practicing random acts of kindness to connect with others, creating a sense of community.

Incorporating this list into my daily life shapes how I feel as a human being, and it increases my focus and sense of accomplishment. I become more conscious of investing my time in a manner that maximizes my energy potential. Once you create your list and start following it, once you consciously spend your 24 hours each day, I believe you will enjoy increased physical energy and operate at a higher level of performance and productivity. You will alter your perception of time and change how you view what you should focus on. And most important, you will live a life of greater joy and presence. So, I ask you, what are the ten things by which you will organize your 24 hours?

OUTSOURCE YOUR LIFE, INSOURCE YOUR PASSION

There are some things that are perfectly egalitarian on this planet. Birth and death, for example. And the fact that in between, we each have 24 hours per day of our life. The President of the United States gets 24, I get 24, and you get 24. But as our lives get busier, as juggling schedules becomes more challenging, and as our options increase, it becomes increasingly difficult to do everything we want to in 24 hours. So we lead frenzied, busy lives, lurching from one commitment to another under the tyranny of schedules.

When my life became too crazy and I was dropping balls right and left, I stumbled upon a concept that shifted my paradigm. I discovered the concept while reading an A. J. Jacobs article in *Esquire,* "My Outsourced Life." Corporations outsource, he pointed out, so why not individuals? After reading the article, I realized that we can "buy" time in a free market capitalist economy and, as a result, extend our days to 28 or 32 or 36 hours.

I became truly inspired when Timothy Ferriss, author of the bestseller *The 4-Hour Work Week: Escape the 9–5, Live*

Anywhere, and Join the New Rich, spoke at Google. His compelling logic is as follows: Take your annual salary and divide it by 2,000 hours, which is the average number of hours people in America work in a year. The resulting number is the economic value of an hour of your time based on your current compensation. Let us say your current hourly compensation is $40. If there is something you need to get done and it is not your area of expertise—or not your passion—and someone else can do the job for you for less than you earn per hour ($40, in this example), then you could consider giving the job to them.

Say you've calculated your earnings to $40 an hour, which is the same hourly rate you might pay for someone to build a deck or paint your house or help you cook for a party. The job is not in your skill set, so it would take you twice as long as a professional, and your end product wouldn't be nearly as good. In that case, it makes sense to outsource, and you could spend the time you save focusing on what refuels you—meditating, mountain bike riding, or decluttering your closet.

Actually, we all outsource to a greater degree than we realize. Ferriss argues—and his reasoning had a major effect on me—that the majority of us already outsource much of our lives. We've already turned over so many tasks to others, and we've been doing so for years. Take the food we eat, for example. Ninety percent of the food my grandparents consumed they grew, harvested, and prepared themselves. The rice, the bananas, the coconuts, the vegetables, the milk from the cow that stood in the cowshed behind the house—everything, except a few staples from the local store, came from their farm. Now, if I look at my own life or the life of any of my friends, we grow and harvest zero percent of our food. And in my case, because I am so often away from home, I don't prepare my food either. Maybe on weekends, when I am home, I will cook something, but by and large, I don't do it. If I had to grow, harvest, and cook all the food I eat, I would be dead in three days.

Ferriss convinced me to take a closer look at the idea of outsourcing. So I read his book, followed through, and tried a few of his ideas, plus some of my own. For example, I have a personal assistant in India through the virtual assistant service GetFriday. Nisha sits in Bangalore but can handle anything that can be done on the phone or web. For example, if I am going on vacation, she will stop my mail and all my subscriptions. A few years ago, someone broke into my car and stole my navigator. Nisha arranged for a repair shop to come to my office in the San Francisco Bay Area and replace the glass, and then she ordered a new navigator on the web. Those calls might have taken 45 minutes of my time, which would be difficult to find in a work day. So I wouldn't have been able to fix my window, replace my navigator, or drive my car for several weeks.

Some might look at outsourcing as exploitation, but Nisha charges the same hourly rate as a personal assistant in the United States does. However, because her company specializes in providing assistance to international clients 24/7—each assistant working with multiple clients—it has developed highly optimized systems, which makes her incredibly efficient and, in the end, less expensive.

Silvia and Azha, my personal assistants, are geniuses at making order out of chaos. In my house, stuff accumulates over time, especially when I travel. Piles of books, mail, photos, gifts, and bills cover my desk, kitchen counter, and dining table. Either Silvia or Azha comes in for a couple of hours one or two weekends a month. Together, we work around my home office, and in two hours—no more clutter. Clean surfaces. Junk mail tossed, bills paid, important papers filed, and my to-do items neatly sorted in two small folders labeled "Urgent" and "Medium Priority." The psychic energy cost of a cluttered office is tremendous. But with just a few hours of teamwork, I am done with home office work for another two weeks, until stuff piles up again.

Because of their system, I can quickly find my Cesária Évora CD or the receipt for the music system I bought two years ago and need for warranty repairs. And I don't have to go through the embarrassment I went through when I returned from a speaking engagement in Copenhagen and found that my car battery had died, which in turn activated the antitheft feature on my car stereo. When I took my car to the dealer to reactivate the stereo, he asked for my secret code. I had it somewhere, printed on a card from the manufacturer, but I had no idea where it was. I checked my glove compartment, my wallet, but I couldn't find it, and I ended up paying $300 to listen to my music in my car. A year later, after I implemented my declutter system with Silvia, the manufacturer's card miraculously appeared from a pile of papers in my home office. Now the card's neatly filed away under "Car," where I can easily retrieve it.

Thanks to globalization, technologies, and new business models, you can take advantage of services such as Nisha's and Azha's at a much lower rate than you would expect. For example, take a look at TaskRabbit, the online and mobile service, where you can outsource small jobs and tasks. You post the job and the price you're willing to pay, and a network of preapproved TaskRabbits in your neighborhood bid for the job. It's a brilliant idea that would not have been possible without smartphones, the Internet, and online rating and payment systems.

To me, outsourcing is similar to going through my in-box. I file some items to deal with later, delete some items, and focus on what's most important and on where I can be the most productive. And that doesn't necessarily mean in my work. I teach free yoga lessons and have done so ever since I trained to be a yoga instructor in India. This is my gift to the world. By consciously choosing to pay someone to take care of tasks that are not my passion or my skill set, I gain two hours a week when I can teach yoga, which *is* my passion and aligns with my five essentials, for free. If I tried to manage my website myself, I would be terrible at it. Much better to take that time for what's essential to me: to indulge my passion and offer my gift, both of which bring me, and I hope others, great joy.

FRIEND YOURSELF

We all brag about how many people friend us on Facebook or follow us on Twitter. When people want to connect with us on LinkedIn, half the time we don't even know how we know them. If there's someone we'd like to get to know or pull into our business network, we can go on the Internet, search for that person by name, and connect. I have more than 20,000 followers on Google+ alone. Very few of them are my friends. Most of them I don't even know. And most of them don't know me. Yet if I post a blog on the *Huffington Post* website, if I notify all my social media connections, I can easily get that blog into the hands of 20,000 people, I can ask them to read it, and many of them will.

There's no doubt social media technologies are allowing us to connect on a scale we couldn't have imagined before. I couldn't handwrite letters to 20,000 people, but with a few keystrokes, I can send a message to all of them at once. And theoretically, all 20,000 could send their own messages to me. I often speak about the estimated 7 billion mobile cellular connections on the planet. I ask the audience to assume for a minute that each one of these devices is in the hands of a different member of our human family of 7.2 billion people. Based on that assumption, all 7 billion of us could conceivably connect with one another.

That's amazing, but in the midst of this relentless social engagement, this all-encompassing connectivity, we can lose ourselves in the rhythm of other people's lives, in what is of interest to them. Social media isn't a passive activity. It's interactive. We engage, post a comment, retweet, like, accept an invitation.

I admit, I get caught up. I can start out with the best intentions. Maybe I need to send out a quick e-mail before I go to bed, and just as I press "Send," I receive a notification that Lorenz, who's on vacation in Bali, has just posted a picture of the Ubud Monkey Forest. Then another e-mail comes through, with a comment about Lorenz's picture: "Oh, amazing. You should really check out Merta Sari restaurant in Pesinggahan." Then someone else joins the conversation: "My most vivid memory of Bali was the BaliSpirit Festival." Moments later, another post: "Me too. Fantastic music and dancing. Take a look at these videos." And I have some interest in that style of music and dance, so I click through to the video, and now all of a sudden I'm drawn in. I just logged in to answer an e-mail, and 30 minutes later, I'm watching videos of people from all over the world decked out in yoga pants and twirling Hula-hoops around their waists, hips, and thighs.

It happens to most of us. It's natural. We set out to do one thing and we get sucked into another. The mind is like a monkey, zipping from A to Q, distracted by shiny objects. Curious.

As human beings, we all possess the tendency to be distracted. So with social media, we can expect our attention to wander, to get sucked into the social vortex, pulled toward responding to invites, reviewing status updates, and checking messages. Our minds can get full, our lives can get full—overfull—and in the process, we can neglect ourselves. So we need to step back.

A friend of mine, Cari Widmyer, sometimes goes cold turkey. In the evening, when she comes home from work, she turns off all electronics, anything she uses for communication—her laptop, her cell phone, her electronic reader—and locks them up in the trunk of her car, which she parks in the garage of her building. If Cari's overwhelmed by a pressing concern, she has to leave the house, walk down a flight of stairs, go into the garage, open the trunk of her car, and grab her laptop or her phone. So unless there's a huge urgency, she leaves her electronics in the car until she finishes her morning practice.

Maybe such a radical disconnect isn't your style or seems too severe. So instead you could step back by scaling back, saying to yourself: *I'm not going to have more than 200 connections on any one form of social media,* or *I'm going to spend only one hour looking at social media.* Or maybe you turn off all the push functionality, so you're aware of activities only when you choose to log in to your account and check.

Or you may choose to just walk away from technology for a while, take a short break from the rhythm of other people's lives and tune in to your own. You can check into some wildly philosophical paradisiacal retreat, or you can just focus on something as simple as noticing how you feel in your body, paying attention to the flow of your energy. Go for a bike ride, take a walk, show up for yoga class, sit down and meditate, or do something that lifts you up (for me, it's savoring a cup of spicy, milk-laced masala chai)— anything that gives you an opportunity to turn away from all of these external connections and focus on the deep, internal connection with yourself, that place where you really know yourself.

It's amazing that we have all these relationships with people around the world, and social networking technologies make it extremely easy, but in the middle of all this connectivity and sharing and radical transparency and hyper-relationship-building we need to remember that the most important relationship we can have is the one with ourselves. So here's my recommendation. Take a tip from the enormous potential for outward connectivity social media provides, and turn that same connectivity inward. Take the time to friend yourself, listen to the tweet of your heartbeat, pay attention to the status update from your body, and respond to the urgent chat request from your brain. As Lao-tzu wrote in *The Way of Life,* "He who knows others is wise; he who knows himself is enlightened." We can do both.

PART III

OPTIMIZE YOUR SYSTEM

An optimized computer performs at maximum efficiency, all systems working simultaneously, seamlessly, in parallel. Our success as humans—mysterious, miraculous orchestra of interdependent systems that we are—hinges on building practices and habits to optimize the way we function in day-to-day life. We do this so we can live our lives in the most coherent and conscious way we're able, so we're running at peak capacity, maximum performance, and top productivity on all levels—spiritual, emotional, physical, and mental. It takes dedication. It takes practice.

In his book *Outliers: The Story of Success*, Malcolm Gladwell writes of such dedication, proposing what he calls the "10,000-hour rule": the amount of time we need to practice a craft before we master it. From the Beatles to Bill Gates to Yo-Yo Ma, behind their success is at least 10,000 hours of sawing away on the cello somewhere in a basement that the world does not see. This is the hard work of preparing for the magic, tilling the soil and getting the ground ready for the bloom to happen with what seems to be a seamless, effortless grace.

YOUR WORDS
HAVE POWER

What goes through your mind when the phone rings at two o'clock in the morning? Most of us think it's bad news, and some of us think it is *People* magazine calling to tell us we have been voted Sexiest Person Alive.

This time, it was neither. It was my friend Dr. Babu Ramachandran. He was calling from Bahrain in the Middle East, and he had quite a story.

It had all begun 12 years earlier. I was visiting my hometown in India, and I had a delightful surprise. You know how it feels when you go home and find out that a friend you have not seen in ten years is also back? So it was: my dear old friend Babu was visiting. He had gone on to become a famous doctor and was working in Bahrain.

We decided to meet at the old Mascot Hotel, which when we were growing up represented the height of luxury. Western tourists and business executives from the big cities stayed there. As high-school students we would ride our bicycles past the hotel and enviously look into the gardens, past the guard at the gate and the waiters in the garden wearing turbans styled like Japanese paper fans. It was all meant to convey the luxurious lifestyle of an Indian maharajah. We thought it looked silly to go to work dressed like that. But now, as professionals working internationally and earning an income in dinars and dollars, we felt as if we could confidently walk into the Mascot Hotel and act like maharajahs for a day. We talked about the dreams we'd had growing up, the lessons we had learned in life, the girls he had kissed and I had failed to kiss and what had become of them.

Suddenly Babu became introspective. "Gopi, as a doctor I treat sick people one at a time," he said. "I feel I can have a bigger impact by speaking to large audiences and teaching them how to stay healthy, rather than treating a few patients after they are already sick. But I am simply not a public speaker. I am afraid of being a leader on a big stage. I am at an impasse." Then he was quiet.

I sat there quietly for a while, and then I smiled. "Babu, do you remember the high-school speaking club you ran at the YMCA? Do you remember that is where we first met and I could barely string a few sentences together before I would turn beer brown"—as Indians it is impossible for us to turn red—"and sit down in embarrassment? Last year I made it to the semifinals of the World Championship of Public Speaking."

Babu's look was that of someone who had just seen an elephant from Kerala walk into the gardens of the Mascot Hotel and order a cup of masala chai from the waiter wearing the turban styled into a Japanese fan.

"Have you heard of Toastmasters, Babu?"

"What is Toastmasters, Gopi? It sounds like a drinking club."

"Well, Babu, given that the club I belong to at Stanford University goes for drinks and dinner on University Avenue after each meeting, you could call it a drinking club with a speaking problem! But seriously, it is like an

Your Words Have Power

Alcoholics Anonymous for people who fear public speaking. You should check it out. It will change your life."

That same day I Googled it and found out that there was a Toastmasters club in Bahrain. Just a single club at that time for the whole country, in the capital, Manama. I encouraged Babu to visit the club.

Then we both got busy with our lives, and for the next four years I heard nothing from Babu. Until the night when my phone rang at 2 A.M. I grabbed it with sweaty hands, fearing the worst.

"Hello, who is it? Is there a problem?"

"Hey, Gopi!" a cheery voice said. "This is Dr. Babu. How is sunny California? I just had a quick question. Are you close to Reno, Nevada?"

If the phone had been a club, I would have clobbered him. Either Dr. Babu now had a drinking *and* gambling problem or he was organizing the world's greatest bachelor party.

"Yes, I am close by," I responded. "But why are you asking me this at 2 A.M.?"

"So sorry, Gopi," Babu replied. "I miscalculated the time difference. The Toastmasters International convention is in Reno. I plan to attend, and I want you to be there with me."

Now I was really mad. For this he woke me up—to tell me he was attending a Toastmasters convention—as if it was an invitation to the Oscars?

And then Babu told me the whole story.

Babu had returned to Bahrain, followed my advice, and joined Toastmasters. He had worked through the program and reached a fairly high level of proficiency, a kind of black belt in the public speaking world. Then he decided to enter an international speaking contest—and became the world champion in his category. The simple suggestion I'd made to him during our talk four years earlier had had a huge impact on his life. That was why he wanted me with him in Reno—to share in what he had accomplished.

When Babu walked across the stage at the international convention to receive his award, my heart soared. I know Babu was proud. But I was the proudest man in that room. I was beaming. Here was someone who had never done any public speaking, who spoke English as a second language, who had concluded that he had stopped growing. And now he was receiving one of the greatest recognitions in the world of public speaking.

Last month my phone rang again at 2 A.M. It was Dr. Babu—of course! "Gopi," he said excitedly, "I want you to come to Bahrain in April. It is the tenth anniversary of Toastmasters in Bahrain. I am the district governor"—the highest office in a Toastmasters district—"and I want you to deliver the keynote at the celebration. My life changed in a profound way. I owe it to you."

Now it was my turn to look like a man who had seen an elephant walk in and order masala chai from a waiter at the Mascot Hotel. What I was most incredulous about was this. I had made the tiniest of suggestions—"You should check it out." But he had followed through and it had gone on to launch his career as a medical professional using the stage as a platform to address public health issues and making an entire country healthy thousands of people at a time.

We don't realize the amount of power that words carry. Of course, the words that come out of the mouth of a Jesus or Buddha or Gandhi or Mandela have gone on to change the life trajectory of billions of people, freed up entire societies, and shifted the course of history. Gandhi's response to the British, "An eye for an eye will only make the whole world blind," made everyone sit up and commit themselves to a more nonviolent way of revolution. Martin Luther King Jr.'s "I have a dream" inspired an entire generation to fix what wasn't working, and to do it with a determined focus on peaceful change.

But I don't think we realize that our normal conversations with friends, family, or mentees pack that kind of power. That five words chosen carefully, as mine to Dr. Babu were, may be all it takes to put someone on the road to a world championship stage. Dr. Babu taught me to be more thoughtful about what I tell people. Especially in mentoring conversations. To be aware of the kind of impact it could have on someone's life in years to come. To realize that a collection of phonetics, depending on how they're strung together, can have a tremendous impact. They can hurt or denigrate or invigorate or inspire. They can, in fact, affect an entire system. That choice is available to us every time we open our mouths.

THE PRACTICAL VEGETARIAN

I am a practical vegetarian. In a world where vegetarians are already marginalized, and fringe groups are further subcategorized as vegans, pescatarians, raw foodies, lacto-ovo vegetarians, and on and on, I have invented a new category.

A practical vegetarian is someone who almost always eats plant-based food when that choice is available. And when that choice is not available, she is open to eating whatever food is indeed available and doing so with gratitude. The difference between being a strict vegetarian as opposed to a practical vegetarian is the world of difference between easily following a kind diet and struggling to stick to a rigid regimen.

Strangely, when growing up in India, where it was easy to be a vegetarian, I was a meat eater; now, living in the United States, where it is easy *not* to be a vegetarian, I have chosen to be a practical vegetarian. Part of the reason is that it took time and a shifting of consciousness to really understand the virtues of eating mostly plant-based food. As Gabriel García Márquez wrote in *Love in the Time of Cholera,* "Wisdom comes to us when it can no longer do any good." Over time, the wisdom sunk in. And I must confess that Alicia Silverstone's talk at Google on her book *The Kind Diet: A Simple Guide to Feeling Great, Losing Weight, and Saving the Planet* was a tipping point. She spoke about the benefits of eating more plant-based foods, such as clear skin, great energy, better digestion, and easier weight management. But what really struck me was when she talked about how eating more plant-based foods can positively impact the planet, while eating more animal-based products may have the opposite effect.

It was easy to embrace the virtues of vegetarianism. If you're part of the yoga and consciousness community, you may be all too familiar with these and not need repetition. The impressive and long list includes lower body weight, reduced cholesterol, and lower risk of developing cancer and other diseases. In addition, the livestock industry is one of the largest contributors to environmental damage: air and water pollution, land degradation, climate change, loss of biodiversity. But being a global citizen, a professional in the tech industry with a passion for travel, and a rootless nomad of sorts has meant that I have had to adapt or die. The last few years have taken me to 44 different countries as far apart as Iceland, Mongolia, and Bahrain. In Mongolia, outside of the capital, Ulan Bator, boiled mutton seemed to be the only item on any menu in any restaurant. In Buenos Aires, my business school classmate laid out the most delicious food he had lovingly prepared to make up for the ten years we had not seen each other—empanadas stuffed with minced beef. And on the long-haul United flight returning from a day of meetings in New York, when the attendant came to the last row, where I sat hungry and tired, all she could offer me was a turkey sandwich.

And so it is that I have adapted to survive. I eat only plant-based food when I have the choice in front of me. And I gratefully eat whatever is in front of me when I don't have the choice.

Here are my tips for being a practical vegetarian:

Eat plant-based foods. Do this as much as you can when you have the choice. And eat them as close to their natural state as possible. If you can point to something on your plate and see that it is a carrot or an eggplant or a bean, that is excellent. And if it is not cooked or processed in any way, you are in dietary heaven. We are fortunate at Google, where the chefs in our cafés lovingly lay out a wonderful spread of plant-based food to choose from—often from farms within 150 miles of the campus and sometimes even grown on the Google campus.

Put color on your plate. Nature has done a pretty good job of building the right signals into us. A plate that is exploding in naturally occurring greens and reds and pinks and purples is visually appealing. But it is also likely a healthy plate with a balanced set of nutrients you need.

Choose and eat consciously. Put things on your plate mindfully. Be conscious of what plants, fruits, and vegetables you are choosing. Be conscious of how much or how little you need to feed your body and your taste buds. And eat mindfully too. Be aware of the taste, texture, and smells of the food you eat. Be conscious of the natural goodness and life energy that is packed into that crunchy lettuce, juicy carrot, and sweet grape.

Eat with an attitude of gratitude. The simple truth is that each plate of food in front of me has involved about 60 people whom I will never meet. The person who planted the crop, the person who fertilized the field, those who picked the crop, transported it, chopped it, cooked it. Most of them were toiling away in jobs less comfortable than mine—and doing jobs I am incapable of. I don't know about you, but without these people and their skills I might actually starve to death, unable to grow my own food. I try to remember this and eat thankfully.

Don't beat yourself up—be practical. Having said all this, I also recognize the fact that the dietary choices of others in this world may be different, and that is where the practical aspect comes in. If I don't have a choice of plant-based food, then I am okay with eating animal products. In my book, being vegetarian 96 percent of the time is good enough. I get the health and ecological benefits of a vegetarian diet. It makes my life easier. It makes my host's life easier. And it makes it easy to travel to Arusha, Papeete, Liberia, Ko Samui, Banjul, Tiruchirappalli, Gdansk, Kárahnjúkar . . .

THE TEA BUS

Every day we make choices—and the choices we make can have an impact on others. We have the power to choose what that impact will be. We may choose to be warm, welcoming, and kind or to be cold, indifferent, and rude. In a moment of truth, tell me, which do you choose?

Not long ago, I was excited when my friends Jordan and Kathy accepted my invitation to visit San Francisco. I told them, "Come to our city of love!" I wanted them to have an absolutely fantastic time. We went to a fine restaurant, then a concert at the Fillmore, and to wind down the night we walked into a lounge.

An officious-looking manager blocked us at the door. "Stop! Stop, you can't come in. We're closing."

"But you don't close for another twenty minutes. There are customers still sitting here."

"We are not serving anymore," he snapped. "Please leave. Now!"

I stood there frustrated, wondering, *Why is this manager choosing to be so unwelcoming?* I was sure Jordan and Kathy were thinking, *Gopi, this is your city of love?*

The choices the manager was making in that moment were having an impact on us, no doubt about it.

Suddenly I heard a slurred but friendly voice. "Hey! If you lovely people are looking for a warm place to chill, just go down the street and sit in the Tea Bus."

Tea bus? What was a tea bus? Looking around, I realized that these helpful words were coming from a patron slouched over the bar. I was so embarrassed and desperate, I was ready to take advice from anyone.

"Let's go find this tea bus," I said to my friends.

As we stepped out into the cold, I was sure they were thinking, *Gopi, this is just great. You're going to drag us around San Francisco in search of a* bus? *Because a drunk in a bar told you to? Wow!* But down the block we saw the warm, welcoming glow from—yes—a white bus parked at the curb. We heard the happy sounds of laughter. "Come on, guys," I said. "Let us check it out."

The bus was a refurbished school bus, the short kind, with a big roof rack and side mirrors that stuck out like ears. Inside there was a group of happy people sitting in a circle, sipping warm tea, engaged in animated conversation. And in the midst of it all stood a young man with the most angelic face I had ever seen.

"Hi, my name is Guisepi," he said. "Please join us for some tea. It is warm, refreshing, and free!"

In my surprise I heard his name as Tea Hippie. "Hi, Tea Hippie. I am Tea Gopi. This is Tea Jordan and Tea Kathy."

Kathy looked delighted as we climbed aboard the bus and settled onto wooden benches padded with deep purple cushions. The floor was wood as well, and the bus was even fitted with a woodstove. "This is so cool!" Kathy said. "I've never experienced anything like this back home."

Tea Gopi lifted his chin and said proudly, "Jordan, Kathy, welcome to San Francisco—city of love!"

We took the mugs of tea that Tea Hippie handed around. The tea was warm and refreshing, as he'd promised. As we sipped, I asked him, "Hey, Tea Hippie. Dude. What's your story?"

And Tea Hippie responded.

"A few years ago I was disillusioned with my life. To make a change, I started making pots of tea and loading it on my truck. I'd park in busy neighborhoods and offer it to anyone who wanted a refreshment, or to talk to someone, or just be seen."

You see, he was offering more than tea: company, conversation, community.

Tea Hippie continued. "Everyone related to each other. Sometimes a Japanese tourist, or a tattooed gangster, or a shopkeeper. Everyone was comfortable sitting at the same level, drinking a warm cup of tea, and connecting. In return, they were inspired to do small acts of kindness in their own lives." Before he knew it, the Free Tea Party was born.

At some point the truck was exchanged for the white bus, whose name, we learned, was Edna. Her wood was all reclaimed Douglas fir; she had a solar electric system and even running water. And Tea Hippie went on serving tea, financing the endeavor with support from sponsors, donors, and people who pitched in to help or share their resources, as well as out of his own pocket. The free tea was a perfect example of the "gift economy," the idea that goods or services can be offered without expecting anything in return. Guisepi told us, "I realized I could impact the world one person at a time, one cup of warm tea at a time."

There it was again: the choices we make, the impact we choose. And I asked myself: could I choose to do something—something small and good—that would impact someone's life?

Every day, in everything we choose to do, there is a moment of truth. A choice we make. An opportunity to touch someone's life. Sometimes I do it in small ways. I have made it a point to actually see the "invisible" workforce at Google. The janitors who come in late at night, the security guards around the campus, the chef team that works inside the kitchen and occasionally steps out. I learn their names and talk to them, knowing who they are and some details of their lives. All I am doing is being more present to them.

I also found the answer to my quest in the two most powerful words in our language: *thank you*. The simple act of acknowledging and honoring a contribution that someone around me has made creates a virtuous cycle of feel-good-ness for me and the other person. And it also acknowledges my own interdependency with other people. At the end of each day, no matter how happy or frustrating it has been, I think of someone who has been kind to me in my life, and I simply say thank you. Sometimes I write a card or send a quick e-mail or leave them a phone message. Just the other day I said thank you to Chandrasekhar. I had been traveling in India, and while I was in a small town all by myself, I became very ill. Chandrasekhar, who cleans the rooms at the place where I stayed, helped me see a doctor. I may never see him again. I have no way of contacting him. He does not have a phone or e-mail. So I simply thought of him and thanked him again in my heart. And I know that in some way it must have reached him.

It's as I said: every day we make choices, and our choices make a difference to the people around us. Some may choose an expensive drink. I chose free tea. The manager chose to be inflexible. The drinker chose to be helpful. Tea Hippie chose to be welcoming. I choose to be grateful.

You have choices too—all the time, in every moment. Next time someone cuts in front of you on the freeway, you have the choice to show him one finger or cheerfully wave all five. What choices will you make?

THE BUDDHA
IN THE BOUTIQUE

The first spiritual practice I remember taking part in was the evening ritual at my grandparents' home back in our rice-farming village of Chittilamchery. To honor the sacred hour of sunset, my grandmother and great-grandmother would light an oil lamp and carry the lamp to each doorway to the outside, where they would wave the flames toward the talasi plant, growing on a raised platform, a shrine in front of the house. After they finished, they would sit on the floor on grass mats and sing kirtans for an hour. No traffic, no cars for miles. No refrigerator, no microwave, no dishwasher, no sounds of mechanization at all. Only the chanting. As a five-year-old, I would sit quietly on my grandmother's lap the entire time, rocking back and forth with her, comforted by the rhythm and familiarity of the Malayalam and Sanskrit chants, singing along to learn the words sung in a language I could not read.

I often tell people I feel lucky to have won the ovarian lottery, meaning I feel incredibly blessed to have been born into a culture where practicing meditation and mindfulness have been a part of people's daily lives for hundreds of years, an integral part of the culture and spiritual traditions of that land. In India, we practice meditation to go beyond the mind, beyond the illusion of the physical world, to our divine essence—to be present to that essence in this world. Mindfulness, the fashionable buzzword of the day, is one form of the practice derived from an aspect of that tradition. To be mindful means having your body and mind in the same place and fully present to the activity or experience you are engaged in during this tiny slice of life called *now*. The tiny slice that is really where our life is lived.

Right now, there's a lot of interest in meditation and mindfulness, for which I'm extremely grateful. Unlike the idea of meditation I grew up with—to go beyond the mind—mindfulness meditation focuses on training our minds as we would train our bodies for a bike race, only the goal is to increase not physical endurance but emotional intelligence, as well as cognitive function, clarity, and focus. I'm incredibly thankful for the research of the past 20 years that has grabbed the attention of those in the data-driven world of engineering and business, where people are embracing meditation because of its scientifically proven benefits. We now have proof that meditation can lower your blood pressure, blood sugar, and cholesterol. Meditating can reduce anxiety, encourage healing, and increase the thickness of your cerebral cortex, which is the part of the brain associated with attention, sensory processing, memory, perception, and even your threshold for pain.

For years, much of the field of science has been grounded in what can be physically measured and objectively evaluated, which has been invaluable. That's how we found out about gravity, microorganisms, and better ways to make steel. Today, I see some of our most brilliant scientists working with equally brilliant teachers of meditation—Jon Kabat-Zinn, Matthieu Ricard, and Yong-ey Mingyur Rinpoche—to apply solid evidence to what was previously thought to be intangible.

One of the most well known of these early teachers, and a scientist in his own right, was Siddhartha Gauta-ma, or the Buddha. Interestingly, 2,600 years after describing the eightfold path, he has become the image of all things mindful. A few months ago, I was walking through SoHo in New York when I paused to look at a display in a shop window. There, in the midst of the $3,200–$32,000 Gucci python and crocodile totes and the $1,295 Manolo Blahnik suede lace ankle boots, sat a statue of the smiling Buddha, suggesting a well-considered purchase and the promise of inner peace. From the blissful look on the Buddha's face, shoppers could see he was having a good time. Who wouldn't, surrounded by those $25,000 handbags and beautiful women? After that, I began to see the Buddha popping up every now and then—helping to sell accessories in a shop in a luxury hotel in San Francisco, a department store in Chicago . . .

The Buddha didn't have the kind of technology available today. He had only the power of observation and subjective evaluation. He experimented with his breath and his focus until he cut through the noise, discovered the tools essential to allow his mind to stop racing and settle down. The practitioners and teachers who followed him, who experimented with their own minds and bodies, left tiny footprints for us to follow on our way forward. These early scientists spent hours, years, lifetimes looking inward to the fascinating vast powers of our mind, our consciousness, however you define that intangible inner terrain. They directed their attention to what they could not touch, feel, or physically see in front of them, a meta-mental focus to go beyond the thinking process that takes place during moments of stillness.

That thinking process can sometimes be tough to get around. During my last ten-day silent retreat meditation (that's correct—ten days of total silence, 14 hours out of 24 each day spent in meditation, no reading, writing, music, or even eye contact with another person but the teachers), my mind repeatedly returned to a recent quarterly performance rating that no one in the world remembered or cared about, but clearly stuck in my mind like a stubborn piece of popcorn caught in my teeth. It wasn't the goal, but absolutely part of the process.

In recent years, scientists using advanced technology have proven what the Buddha and his practitioners have known for thousands of years: mental discipline and meditative practice can change how our brain works. We can actually enhance brain function and reach different levels of awareness. In his studies on meditation, Richard Davidson, a neuroscientist at the University of Wisconsin, has found that the mental training of mindful meditation can change the inner workings and circuitry of the brain, perhaps permanently.

Davidson conducted a study with eight of the Dalai Lama's monks. These guys were meditation rock stars. Each one had clocked 10,000 to 50,000 meditation hours over a period of 15 to 40 years. Wired with electrodes, the monks went into deep mindful meditation on unconditional compassion, setting off an electrical storm of gamma waves, which can heighten awareness, focus, memory, self-control, learning, and processing speed. They also increase activity in the left prefrontal cortex, the area of the brain associated with self-control, happiness, and compassion, and reduce activity in the amygdala, which is associated with fight or flight.

The poor Buddha, despite being hip, cool, and trendy now, knew the power that meditation had on the mind and emotions, but without electrodes or gamma-wave-sensing machines that could peer into the left prefrontal cortex, he didn't have a scientific leg to stand on. He just observed. He could say only, "I notice you are happier," or "I notice you have greater clarity."

In his internationally best-selling book *Search Inside Yourself*, my close friend and fellow Googler Chade-Meng Tan writes of the benefits of mindful meditation: "Your mind becomes increasingly focused and stable, but in a way that is relaxing. It is like balancing a bicycle on easy terrain. With enough practice, it becomes almost effortless, and you get the experience of moving forward and being relaxed at the same time."

Mindfulness takes me to a state of stillness, where I am able to function better at any task I am doing or any mental process I have to go through. If I have to create a complex spreadsheet, or analyze data, or strategize about how to solve a difficult business problem, I can tackle the problem with greater clarity and focus, one step at a time. A few rounds of sun salutations on my mat can do it. Or a few minutes of sitting on my cushion and repeating my mantra. Or something as simple as taking a pen and a white sheet of paper, sitting in a quiet room, and writing down the first creative solution that comes to me.

Imagine you're trying to work through a complex mental task and you're in the middle of Times Square, with all its noise and commotion and confusion, with so much to see, so many distractions coming at you from all directions, that even if you're standing still in the midst of the activity around you, it's difficult to think clearly. But if you walked into the DoubleTree or the Westin hotel, booked a room, and sat by yourself with no distractions— no TV, no music, no conversation buzzing—you could work through the issue quickly.

Meditation works the same way as checking into the Westin. Most of the time our minds are the equivalent of Times Square—thoughts of the past, present, and future racing and careening and flashing and honking, interrupted by social media messages popping up on our phones and computers, an ad on TV, a headline shouting from the newspaper on the coffee table, or a cookie crumb on the floor that we need to sweep up. Meditation allows us to just drop into a state of stillness, a space with less clutter, so we can bring our minds to what is truly important.

It's the mental equivalent of taking a glass of water from a river or a lake. The water is muddy, but if you allow it to sit still for a while, the sediment settles, and the water nearer the top of the glass becomes very clear, transparent. You can see through it. Something similar happens when we still our minds, when we sit down for meditation and let the sediment of thought settle gradually into clarity.

Now, of course, modern-day gurus preach mindful meditation to increase productivity and creative thinking at work. The idea is that in that state of stillness, you can bring clarity to bear on thorny business problems, arriving at a better solution. The purists might cringe a little at using meditation for worldly commercial purposes. After all, meditation is at heart a spiritual practice, a tool to cut through the ordinariness of this world to get to what is really the essential truth in our lives. But having said that, if you still want to use mindfulness to increase your sales quota, that's fine too. At least you're now meditating regularly. The Buddha is not going to complain about that goal—he is himself selling handbags in the Gucci store, of course with nonjudgmental self-awareness. Why is he sitting there otherwise?

As I'm sitting at my computer, mindfully focused on writing about meditation and tuning out distractions, the bigger mastermind of my life pops up on the screen in front of me, obliterating my concentration. With traffic, it seems, I'll need 46 minutes to get to Greg and Amy's party if I follow the outlined route. One of the Google processes must be picking up the event on my calendar and flashing a map, showing me how to get to the party without being so late that I offend my hosts. I have plenty of time, but just for a second, I'm reacting: *Oh my God, I have got to get to this party. Forget about meditation. I have to run.* And this pop-up illustrates my point. One distraction can bust your focus, your practice, send you flying to the car and racing to whatever comes next.

But it doesn't have to. With your increased sense of focus, you're still going to become distracted, but you can bring yourself back to the task at hand more quickly. So, for example, after receiving the pop-up, I closed my eyes and focused on my breath for two minutes. And my mind returned to what I was working on.

Meditation techniques can range from the simple yet mindful focus on your breath, or even on the taste of chocolate as it melts inside your mouth, to the more complex methods learned from years of study with your spiritual teacher. It all depends on which way you choose to go. You can practice mindful exercises anywhere: I often practice on a plane, in a conference room, and in front of my computer terminal. Or if you have the time and inclination, and want to go deep within for an extended period, you can attend a ten-day retreat, as I've done, where you meditate 14 hours a day and speak to no one the entire time, where you live in complete silence, with no eye contact, no reading, no writing—no stimulation. Just you and your thoughts. The entire time. It can be challenging.

But to get back to the basics. The goal of mindful meditation is to gain clarity and focus, so you can arrive at more creative solutions with any business problem or anything that is going on with your life. More important, once you clear the clutter, you can get to what's called the source of truth about your life and what is going on in it. As Radhanath Swami says, "Just creating people who can earn, who can invent, is not going to help the world in itself unless people become holistic, unless people become united with their own inner spiritual nature and act with dynamic compassion in this world on that basis."

In India, you find reminders of the spiritual everywhere—altars and shrines honoring a whole range of religious beliefs and teachings on the dashboards of taxis, in traditional stores, in hotels. These reminders were such a part of my life that I never noticed them until I'd moved away and came back to visit my family. I miss them. When I see the Buddha while indulging in a bit of shopping in SoHo, checking into a hotel, or racing to catch a flight, his presence reminds me to pause, step back, and reconnect with what is truly important—the sacredness and meaning inherent in this tiny slice of life called *now*.

ONE MINUTE OF MEDITATION, ONE MINUTE OF YOGA

I'm 19 years old, sitting in Padmasana, Lotus Pose, under the thatched roof of an outdoor yoga practice deck. Legs crossed, eyes closed, I breathe in the fragrance of coconut, jasmine, and banana, feel the warm breeze drifting from the lake. As I focus on my breathing, I'm faintly aware of the water lapping the shore, the temple bells ringing, and a cow mooing in the distance as a farmer walks it from the field for its milking. I could stay here forever, but soon I will be graduating from the yoga teacher training program and leaving the Sivananda Ashram in Neyyar Dam, Kerala, India.

For the past month, I've felt I've had some sort of integrity toward a regular practice. Every morning, along with 119 fellow students from around the world, I've awakened at dawn, moving promptly into half an hour of meditation, followed by kirtan singing, morning *satsang,* and two hours of yoga. In the evening, we reverse the order—two hours of yoga, meditation at 8 P.M., and then kirtan singing, followed by evening *satsang.* The mental and physical discipline has changed me, transformed me inside and out in an amazing way. With every breath, I feel the power of what is possible.

I'm excited, living in a more elevated state than I have ever known in my short 19 years of life. At the same time, my mind is much quieter. It's magical what four hours of yoga and one full hour of meditation a day have done. As I walk through the gates of the ashram and down the hill, my backpack strapped to my back, I make a commitment to myself. To maintain this amazing energy outside the walls of the ashram, I'm going to practice yoga for an hour and meditate for 30 minutes. Every day.

I kept my vow for two days—yes, days, not months—after I left the ashram. By day three my grand plan for my life had completely collapsed. After that, I rarely met my commitment. As a college student, my commitment to my practice shifted to a commitment to staying up until 2 A.M., drinking masala chai, and listening to Jimi Hendrix or Led Zeppelin—all because we wanted to be cool and hip.

As the years went on, business school demanded all my focus, and later at McKinsey & Company, and then Google, business meetings, travel, and long hours ate up my days. The only time I could find the structure, the rhythm of life, that supported me was when I went back to one of the Sivananda Ashrams in Neyyar Dam, Grass Valley, or the Bahamas, or when I visited my spiritual teacher Rama Devi's spiritual community in Mangalore. While on retreat, I'd spend two hours twice a day in yoga class. I'd meditate for 30 minutes in the morning and 30 minutes in the evening. I'd come back to myself, feeling centered, feeling grounded, and, most important, feeling I had an integrity toward my practice and a sense of control through somehow reining in my mind.

But only while I was on retreat. Other than my time at retreats, the commitment felt impossible. For years I struggled, and for years I felt a massive sense of failure. One day, about four years ago, I was at work at Google. I had not meditated or practiced yoga for days. I was telling my friend Meng, who has a lot more wisdom than I have, about my struggle.

"Gopi," he said, "why don't you start with one breath? Because an hour of meditation is about six hundred breaths strung together, and you have to get past the first breath and the second before you get to the six hundredth."

Since I am a compulsive, neurotic overachiever, I told him that I was going to do better than that. I was going to commit to a full minute of meditation and a full minute of yoga every day. Now most people think this is the most ridiculous, useless idea they've ever heard, because what is the point in doing one minute of yoga? You don't get anything out of that.

But as soon as the words were out of my mouth, as soon as I committed to one minute, something shifted inside me. I felt hopeful. *No matter how busy I am,* I told myself, *I can carve out sixty seconds for meditation and sixty seconds for yoga every day. That's the time it takes to brush my teeth, and I never go about my day without brushing my teeth.* And so I began.

Before I got caught up in the craziness of the day, whether I was traveling or at home, I'd brush my teeth and say to myself, *Let me do one minute of yoga and one minute of meditation,* and I'd jump right into it before the day started. Sure, sometimes when my schedule was too full or I was too tired, I'd think about skipping my practice, but I could never argue convincingly that I didn't have time, so I kept at it. A week went by, then a month, and for the first time in my life, I could confidently, accurately, and honestly say that I practiced yoga and meditation every day.

Of course, I was practicing for just a minute for each or slightly more than a minute. Still, I had kept my word to myself. I had honored my commitment. But something even bigger shifted inside me, as well, something magical. Often, I would sit for one minute of meditation, and it would feel so amazing, so sweet, I would feel so settled inside that I would ask myself, *Where am I rushing to? What is more important than this?* And I would continue to sit for 3 minutes, 10 minutes, and sometimes 30 minutes.

With yoga, after two sequences of Surya Namaskar, Sun Salutation, which is what I fit into the 60-second time frame, I'd often add a series of Virabhadrasana, Warrior Pose. If I wanted to feel easy and graceful, I'd finish with Natarajasana, Dancing Shiva Pose. Or if I felt energetic and vibrant, about to conquer the world, I'd finish with Simhasana, Roaring Baby Lion Pose, which ends with a big roar.

As I've continued my practice, I've become creative. Sometimes at work, I pop into a conference room before or after meetings, shut the door, and meditate for one minute or do one minute of yoga. Right there. At Google, we have plenty of yoga mats everywhere, so conceivably, if I couldn't find a conference room, I could practice yoga in the corridor or on the lawn, and no one would bat an eye. I also practice yoga when I'm traveling. I used to carry my yoga mat on the plane until the airlines limited passengers to one piece of baggage, so now, at every hotel I stay in, I'll grab a towel from the bathroom and lay it on the carpet, and that becomes my yoga mat. Some airports have yoga and meditation rooms, so I can just drop by before I catch my flight and run through a few sequences.

When traveling, I always meditate on the plane. There are about 15 minutes from the moment the plane begins taxiing down the runway until it reaches 10,000 feet, the ceiling below which you can't use even approved electronic devices. That in-between time when the flight attendants have taken their seats, the entertainment system has been turned off, there is no service in the galley, and everyone is quietly sitting and reading, sleeping, settling in—no movement, no sound, only the engines running. There's an almost timeless, mystical quality, when you're literally in the clouds, beyond the reach of all forms of communication. No phone calls, no e-mail, no text messages.

As Matthieu Ricard, French molecular biologist turned Tibetan Buddhist monk, once said, "A flight is a brief retreat in the sky. There is nothing I can do. So it is actually quite liberating. There's nowhere else I can be. So I just sit and watch the clouds and the blue sky. Everything is still and everything is moving. It's beautiful."

It's interesting and strange to me that in my modern life, if I need a moment of respite from electronic communication, I have to be 10,000 feet above the ground, in the clouds, on a plane. It's one of the few places left on the planet—they even have Internet on Mount Everest—where you're unreachable. So I take that time, those 15 minutes in the clouds, and I meditate.

The idea of one minute of mindfulness has changed my life. I spread the word when I give speeches about moving from the Internet to the inner-net. When I've finished, people come up to me to discuss the one-minute idea, or they send an e-mail, or they post a comment on social media about how profoundly the one-minute plan affected them. Think about it. What if you were to practice at least one minute of mindfulness every day? Whatever

KARMA YOGA AND THE YOGLERS

In Las Vegas, in this most unconscious of cities—where everything is larger than life, from the hotels to the casinos to the entertainment, and visitors take a vow of amnesia (whatever happens in Vegas stays in Vegas)—I lead the entire room, more than 10,000 Googlers, employees from the business side of Google, through a surprise yoga and meditation break. We're at the company's annual business conference in the Vegas-scale expo and convention center. I stand on a 300-foot stage, next to Larry Page, the founder of Google, and other executives, surrounded by Googlers who are yoga enthusiasts. Peering beyond the floodlights, I see thousands of Googlers, on the floor in front of their chairs, spreading out to each side, to the back, occupying every available space. The room is huge, and it's packed.

I face the front of the room. "Take a deep inhale," I say, "and an exhale." I breathe in, then out. "Interlock your fingers and reach for the sky." I turn to the right, addressing the Googlers on the far side of the room. "Balance on your toes and grow an inch taller." I turn to the left. "You are in Tadasana, Mountain Pose, so stand tall and steady like a mountain, and flow with your breath."

Then arms out, hands open, we chant *Om,* a huge crescendo rising, lifting everyone, the radiant energy transforming the entire room. That day we believe we set a record—the largest yoga class ever in the Americas, the third-largest yoga class in the world, based on what we know. A truly magic moment. Breathtaking in scope and scale.

Ever since I can remember, I yearned to immerse myself in yoga, to master postures, *asanas,* and connect to my inner-net. When I was 19, right out of high school, I told my high-school classmates of my plans to study at the Sivananda Ashram in Neyyar Dam, 20 miles from my hometown. They ridiculed me mercilessly. They thought I'd lost it. Yoga had yet to become the craze it is now in the West. It was still an esoteric practice taught mainly in ashrams by bearded men dressed in orange. I didn't blame my friends for giving me a hard time. They were all trying to separate from anything that had to do with our culture, to go toward something else, anything else, just so it was cool. Listening to rock was cool. Studying yoga was not.

Yet I felt that somehow I was born into yoga, and so I left for the ashram in the foothills of the Western Ghats. I stayed there for a month, practicing different aspects of yoga 14 hours per day, singing kirtan, attending *satsang,* meditating. At the ashram, yoga teachers and meditation experts spoke of the gift of this amazing tradition, this lifestyle, the practice of yoga inherited from other great teachers who had gone before us, who hadn't had too much by way of technology or research but had experimented with their minds and bodies and passed that knowledge on to us. Swami Vishnudevananda (one of the people who first brought yoga to America) and Swami Shankarananda, my teachers, taught us yoga as a path to self-realization but also as a practice that brings joy, peace, and happiness to the world. They wanted us to learn and then teach others. I have taught yoga ever since, for free. I will only teach it for free, because this is my gift. The best I can do to serve the people who taught me, and those who taught them, is to pass on their teachings.

When I joined Google, one of my product managers encouraged me to teach a yoga class, and I said yes. I started teaching a class in a conference room to one student and called it Yoglers. I taught every Monday. The class now averages about 20 students.

One day, a year after I started Yoglers, I sat in Charlie's Café at Google with Douglas, a friend of mine, also a teacher in the same traditional lineage. I was bemoaning the lack of students, bouncing ideas off him about how to promote the class, to make it big. "Maybe we need to hold class two nights a week instead of one," he said. "You could teach Mondays, and I could teach Wednesdays."

I hesitated. "You might not get many students."

Then he taught me something profound that has stayed with me since. "I'm going to offer these classes anyway," he said. He wasn't worried about the numbers. It didn't matter to him whether he had 1 student or 30 students. "If only one person shows up," he said, "I'll try to teach that one person with the same amount of sincerity and dedication and pride and joy I would put into my teaching if there were thirty or three hundred in my class. The need to have thirty or three hundred just feeds our own ego."

I reflected on his words and realized that he was right. My ego needed my class to be the largest, the most popular. My ego needed me to be the greatest teacher. I'd lost sight of my real purpose in teaching yoga—to serve the divine. In the yoga practice, there is a concept called karma yoga, one of the four paths of yoga, where you serve selflessly, without feeding your ego. If you serve others, you feel a stronger sense of connection. You ease the sense of separation. You diminish the sense of false identification with this body and your being.

That being the case, I realized I should teach my class with the same amount of reverence and gratitude whether 1 person shows up or 100 show up, because it is the same divine being, showing up in 1 body or 100 bodies. That realization changed my frame of thinking, and now I just teach yoga. Actually, once I let go, the class became really popular. Most days, I run out of mats—it's that packed. Yoglers has become a big movement across Google offices, practicing in offices worldwide. Dozens of Google employees lead yoga programs for other Googlers, and many more are training to teach. I had no idea that something I started with one student would evolve to the level it has.

Teaching has deepened my connection with yoga. Leading my class, watching it catch on, seeing others realize the benefits, and bringing those benefits to a corporation—it's so deeply satisfying. And being able to teach at work? I can't believe my good fortune.

Living in Silicon Valley, working at Google, I'm surrounded by these most amazing technologies. The technological explosion in Silicon Valley, in tech companies all over the world, has made a huge difference in our lives, has changed and is continuing to change life and culture around the planet as we know it. At a very rapid pace. In the midst of this whirlwind, we can feel overwhelmed, disconnected. Yoga is a way we can slow down, check in, and deepen our connection with our inner world, so we can engage and connect more fully and freely with the outer.

People ask me how they can start a yoga or meditation program at work. Anyone can do it. You don't need a budget or vast resources. Just grab a conference room, put up a sign that reads "Random acts of meditation" or "Random acts of yoga," and you're in business. It doesn't matter if ten people show, one person, or only you. Just sit, close your eyes, and start meditating, or strike Virabhadrasana, Warrior Pose. If you just sit for 60 seconds and watch your breath, you have just started a meditation program. Or move into Adho Mukha Svanasana, Downward-Facing Dog, and you have a yoga program. You just need to step forward.

With our information-loaded lives, our increasing need for immediate answers, our expectations of instant service, it might seem that the benefits of yoga are needed now more than ever in the workplace. Maybe so, but the benefits of yoga—the rejuvenation, awareness, peace— have always been important. They were important 50 years ago, 100 years ago, as long as there have been human beings. Yoga and meditation help to create a higher-quality, more conscious human being. And any organization— whether it's a corporation or an educational institution— is staffed and run by human beings. If we incorporate these practices into our working lives, we get along with each other better, make better products, and make choices that will better serve our customers. Test it. Observe.

The Buddha did. Twenty-five hundred years ago, he sat in contemplation, gathering his own empirical evidence through observation—what happened when he sat a certain way, breathed a certain way, held his breath in, let it flow out. Often, I find myself closing my eyes, and I'm back in that room in Las Vegas, observing again that amazing moment when we all came together. More than 10,000 people, arms wide, breathing in, breathing

SLEEPING YOUR WAY TO THE TOP

It's fall, just before sunrise, and I'm lying on my bunk bed in a guest cabin at the Sivananda Ashram Yoga Farm, nestled in the Sierra Nevada foothills. Every year, 15 to 20 Yoglers, members of the yoga group I founded at Google, meet to deepen our yoga practice in a setting similar to what you'd find at a traditional ashram in the small mountain settlements of the Indian Himalayas. Outside, the Karma Yogi walks the hillside, weaving among the guest cabins. "Om Namashivaya," she cries, her voice shrill—ringing her brass bell, calling us to meditation and satsang. "It's five thirty."

The Karma Yogi is a volunteer who practices karma yoga, the yoga of selfless service, by serving in the ashram as unpaid staff. She is ringing her bell as an act of service, but I wish she'd stop. Drawing my sleeping bag closer, I snuggle in and doze off. Fifteen minutes later, she's back again. "Om Namashivaya," she calls, her voice even more strident. "It is five forty-five."

In my sleep-fogged mind, I can almost hear an undertone of *Gopi, I know you are inside. Time to get up. Time for meditation.* Still, I am slow to wake. Tired, even though I have slept for seven hours. Opening my eyes, I scan the room. The bunk beds are empty. The Yoglers have deserted me. Three men, vanished, driven from their beds—I find out later—by my snoring, forced to spend the night in the library, where they could sleep in peace.

Several years later, Google invited a number of sleep experts to speak for our Optimize Your Life program. James Maas, Ph.D., a leading expert on sleep and sleep research, spoke about how sleeping fewer than six hours could stop new information from entering long-term memory. Tony Schwartz, CEO and founder of the Energy Project, discussed the famous lab rat experiments conducted by Dr. Allan Rechtschaffen to demonstrate the lethal consequences of long-term sleep deprivation. During the experiment, sleep-deprived rats developed sores, lost weight despite eating more than usual, and suffered a drop in body temperature. After 32 days, all the rats were dead. The upshot of the experiment is that as we deprive ourselves of sleep—an hour here, a half hour there—we expose ourselves to the same risks as the rats. Of course it's true that we will all die one day, but by depriving ourselves of sleep, we're racing to our cremation.

Dr. William Dement, the world's leading authority on sleep and founder of the world's first sleep laboratory at Stanford University, spoke of his work with Cheri Mah and the members of the men's basketball team. By getting more sleep, they improved their sprint times and their free-throw and three-point shooting accuracy, indicating that sleep extension may enhance athletic performance.

But one presenter especially had a huge impact on my life. Sleep specialist Sina Nader of SWAN Medical Group spoke with me after his talk about my trouble sleeping soundly. Within minutes, Sina said, "I'm pretty sure you have sleep apnea."

"Sleep what?" I asked, incredulous. I'd never heard the term. He told me a bit about the condition, of which my snoring was a symptom, and encouraged me to make an appointment for testing. A few weeks later, after a night of sleeping with electrodes connected all over my body, I was officially diagnosed with sleep apnea. All those years, I'd never even suspected I had a sleep condition. Now I understood why I wasn't feeling rested, no matter how many hours I slept.

In layman's terms, here's how my sleep apnea affected my sleep. Thirty-six times an hour, I would stop breathing. I'd just stop. My breathing apparatus went into panic mode, my brain told the apparatus to calm down and start functioning normally again, and as a result of this signal from my brain, I woke up, not fully, just enough to kick-start my system, then I resumed breathing. Thirty-six "micro wake-ups" an hour wrecked my sleep. Now I'm taking corrective action for the sleep apnea. I have three remedies to choose from: a sleep apnea pillow; a device I insert into my mouth that thrusts my jaw forward, so that I look just like the pictures of Neanderthals I saw in my history books; and a small breathing machine. Of the three devices, the breathing machine works best.

I sleep much better now. At work I'm alert and focused. I'm full of energy, even when traveling. I'm less cranky, and my colleagues don't abandon me at retreats. Of course a good night's rest does come at a price. When I travel, I lug the sleep apnea machine with me, so I can wear it when I sleep in my hotel. It's awkward. A big fat tube runs between the machine and my face and covers my nose like an oxygen mask. When I wear the device and someone sees it, I frighten them because I look as though I'm undergoing some emergency medical procedure. It's not a sexy look. I complain to my doctor that I don't look very attractive with a gas mask on my face. Of course, I can always wear my less cumbersome jaw-extending device (great on the plane), which makes me look like a tourist from the Pleistocene era.

Without that series of lectures, I don't know that I ever would have been diagnosed. So I'm very grateful to Google, and I'm grateful to work in a culture that understands the importance of sleep for performance, productivity, and well-being. Many companies in Silicon Valley are beginning to encourage napping. At Google, we have nap pods, a sort of futuristic helmet/chair created for ideal sleeping conditions. The pods are scattered around the Google campus right next to the work areas. We can reserve a pod the same way we book a conference room for a meeting. When I'm sleep deprived, tired, and feel a drop in my productivity, I book a pod, block out time in my schedule, and settle into the reclining chair. I close the lid and let the ambient rhythms soothe me into a 20-minute sleep. If your workplace doesn't have an area designated for sleeping—which I think is as important as employee gyms and rooms for nursing mothers—see if you can steal off to your car, lock the door of your office, or nab a conference room to grab 20 minutes of sleep.

In his book *Power Sleep*, James Maas, who coined the term *power nap*, suggests taking a nap for 15 to 30 minutes. Thirty minutes is the approximate time it takes for your body to go through the first two phases of sleep. When you nap longer, he says, your body lapses into slow-wave sleep, or deep sleep, and you'll wake up feeling groggy and disoriented, and you might as well nap for an hour and a half, so you can go through a complete cycle.

Even though we are slowly beginning to recognize the importance of sleep and napping, sleep deprivation is a serious problem. We're all trying to work harder, accomplish more, and stay on top of a nonstop flood of information. The global marketplace demands that we be available at all times of the day to jump on a call with a colleague. In my case, when I'm in Silicon Valley, I might be on a call with a colleague in Tokyo at 11 P.M. and another in London at 6 A.M.

Before the modern day invaded our lives, we had the natural rhythm of the sun rising and setting, the sunless night signaling that we needed to sleep, the light signaling it was time to go about the tasks we needed to survive. We built our lives around natural light. Now artificial light illuminates our homes, workplaces, and grocery stores, stretching our days long past sundown, sending us the message that it's time to keep going, not wind down. In our hyperconnected lives, we're inundated with a constant stream of TV, phone calls, e-mails, texts, tweets—24 hours a day, 7 days a week. The result? We're walking around in our sleep, and the toll is enormous. Productivity takes a nosedive, energy fizzles, we can't pay attention, and we're crankier. We all need a good night's sleep. And when I say a good night's sleep, I mean at least eight hours. We need to schedule our lives around sleep, instead of working sleep into our schedules.

I'm always hearing people say, "I'm so busy," or "I have to commute," or "I work with teams in another time zone and have to stay up late to meet with them," and I understand. I've said the same things. I still catch myself saying them. I know it's not always possible to get eight hours of sleep. When I can't, I always take naps. You can always build up to eight hours. Maybe start sleeping eight hours on Friday night, for example, when you're done with presentations and meetings and travel and you can sleep in on Saturday. And on Saturday night, when you can go to bed earlier or sleep in on Sunday. On Sunday, you might go to bed a bit earlier too. Give it a try. After a while, you'll develop a routine.

In Arianna Huffington's 2010 talk at TEDWomen, "How to Succeed? Get More Sleep," she urges women to opt out of the cult of sleep deprivation and lead a new revolution, one based on sleep. Actual sleep. "Women," she says, "we are literally going to sleep our way to the top. Literally." (Thank you, Arianna, for inspiring the title of this chapter.) The phrase caught on. Again. Later she spoke at Google, where she told of her wake-up call, when she fainted from lack of sleep, resulting in a broken cheekbone and five stitches in her right eye. As she recovered, she interviewed dozens of experts in the medical and scientific communities and concluded that getting enough sleep leads to increased productivity and happiness.

Coming of age in the midst of the greatest technological revolution in the history of our planet, my generation believed that we would be the first generation in humanity, the first group of people who could defy the laws of nature and get by with far fewer hours of sleep. We were wrong. Before we can even start making the most of the outer technologies, we need to focus on our inner technology. If there were only one thing we could do to connect with our inner self and deepen our inner journey—*one thing*—that would be to get a good night's sleep.

PART IV

JUST
GOOGLE IT

Mountain climbers operate on the "next ridge" principle. Often they can only see the next ridge they need to reach; then, when they get to that ridge, they can see the ridge beyond it, and so on, until finally they see the summit. They keep going because they know the summit is there, whether they can see it or not. When you step through a door, you may not know what is on the other side. But in your search, you learn to trust the universe and know the right resources will show up.

We operate on the same principle of trust when we search the Internet. Tools like YouTube, Google Maps, and Wikipedia have become so versatile and all-encompassing that it seems there's hardly an information request these systems can't deliver. You could ask how many people actually ran a mile under four minutes the same year Roger Bannister broke the record, and the system will somehow find it for you. You enter your request, you trust, and you get your answer. Maybe not every time, but maybe 95 percent of the time, which is still something of a miracle.

WARMTH IN THE
LAST DESOLATE
WILDERNESS

Antarctica, it is becoming clear to me, is truly at the end of the earth. I have flown from San Francisco, California, to Lima, Peru, to Buenos Aires, Argentina, to Santiago, Chile, to Punta Arenas, Chile, and finally to King George Island in the South Shetlands to arrive on this frozen continent.

Antarctica has always held endless fascination for travelers and explorers. It is the largest wilderness on the planet and is owned by nobody. Despite its abundance of natural and mineral riches, somehow a group of otherwise quarrelsome superpowers has agreed to share the continent and use it only for peaceful and scientific purposes. A land covered by a sheath of ice so thick that you can drill for five miles before you get to the actual continental surface. A brooding mass of land with an ethereal silence, larger than Australia and Europe combined, tucked away out of sight on most maps and globes at the arbitrarily defined bottom of the world. A land of endless sunlight and glistening glaciers during summer and a haunting black night for all of winter.

I have wanted to come here for 15 years, and now my intention has come into being. I have wanted to come partly to reach my goal of visiting all seven continents and partly because there was something haunting and impossible in doing so for a little boy who, when growing up in Kozhikode and Thiruvananthapuram in India, did not know anyone who had even traveled to the Western world. And looking wide-eyed at stunning pictures in the travel books of a local public library was his form of virtual travel.

As our tiny aircraft touches down on a gravel strip, piloted expertly by two retired Chilean Air Force pilots, we are met by a grizzled man with a long white beard looking every bit the Antarctic explorer. If you were making a movie on Ernest Shackleton, this is who Central Casting would send you. But Alejo Contreras Staeding is not just any Antarctic explorer. He is a living legend. For the last 30 years he has spent every summer on Antarctica, making him the one human, living or dead, who has spent the most time on the continent. He has made 17 trips to the South Pole, including one in 1989 when he walked all the way from the Weddell Sea. For 97 days he pushed uphill on cross-country skis along with Indian army officer Colonel Bajaj, all their supplies hauled behind them on sleds.

Alejo has also climbed Mount Vinson Massif, the tallest mountain on Antarctica, 16 times, including 6 times with celebrated climber Rob Hall, who died on the Everest summit (made famous in the book and movie *Into Thin Air*). And if that was not enough, in 1994, Alejo also sailed around the entire continent in a clockwise direction against the wind, something no sane sailor would want to do. One of the people visiting with us is Josephine, Alejo's 22-year-old daughter, who is spending the summer with her dad on the continent. She is a psychology student at the University of Chile in Santiago, and I suggest to her gently that perhaps she should study the psychological makeup of her father and other explorers like him and what gives them their sustaining power.

From the Magellan Strait to the South Pole, when anyone needs help of any kind, from logistics to rescue operations, they seem to call Alejo. They trust Alejo will come through. The Chinese research station is nervous about their vice premier visiting in three days and wants a solution to house the 43-person entourage in case the weather turns bad and they can't fly out. They turn to Alejo. A student expedition from my alma mater, Wharton, needs a large quantity of food and fuel. Alejo has organized it. Late at night, although the midnight sun is still bright in the Antarctic summer, the radio crackles with the call signature "Big Fish," wanting to talk to Alejo. It is a crew member from a private yacht full of rich New York hedge-fund managers sailing around Antarctica, and, without a trace of irony—even in these waters where orca, minke, and humpback whales roam freely—their signature is Big Fish.

Two sailors from the Chilean Navy take us on a Zodiac to a beach at nearby Ardley Island, where there is a huge penguin colony and hatchery. Things look busy in the colony. All the adult penguins I am watching have arrived here after swimming thousands of miles from places like the Falkland and Christmas Islands, and with natural instincts as perfect as a human-built GPS they return to the same place where they nested before. Penguins are monogamous birds, and hopelessly devoted to their young, with Dad or Mom always present and holding their chicks close to their chests with their flippers. When your nest is a pile of rocks on an exposed beach with predators circling overhead, you are a sitting duck, or in this case a sitting penguin. A momentary lapse of attention could mean that your chick would disappear in an instant.

The top of the hill on Ardley Island is packed with resident penguins. A virtual skyline of penguins nesting in a neat row. That is a puzzling decision, especially because there is plenty of space on the beach below. Sure, the view is spectacular, but you are now an even worse sitting penguin with no place to hide your chicks from predators. Moreover, penguins, while graceful swimmers in the water, are terrible walkers. Five million years of evolution and they still have not mastered it. With their fins spread out for balance and their underbellies thrust out, they waddle clumsily around the beach on their webbed feet like two-year-olds lurching drunkenly in their diapers around the living room.

As I look up the hill to a penguin path leading to the top of the ridge, it looks like a freeway at rush hour in Los Angeles. Penguins are waddling up and down ungracefully all day long, heading down to the water to fish, heading back up to relieve their husbands or wives from babysitting duties. Along the way they may stop and exchange news and gossip with a friend passing by, perhaps whispering, scandalized, "Puffy has been hanging out with the hot emperor penguin who just arrived from South Georgia."

Across from Ardley Island on the other side of the bay, a sheet of ice 60 stories tall glistens menacingly. A really massive ice cube that could be five million years old. I want to get close to the glacier, but as the wind whips up, our engine dies. When the Chilean sailors get it restarted, they turn the nose of the Zodiac back to the base. Weather changes quickly in the Antarctic and winds can whip up to a speed of 186 miles per hour. To get us out of the roar of the elements, the sailors take us to the Navy clubhouse, where they serve us hot coffee and biscuits and ceremoniously present us with certificates that show that we landed in Antarctica. New visitors are a welcome relief to them.

Back on King George Island, we get invited to the China research station thanks to Alejo's connection and the fact that one of our small group is a venture capitalist from Beijing. The newly built station and aptly named Great Wall Base is breathtaking in scale and impressive in its organization, a beehive of activity with young Chinese geologists, meteorologists, biologists, and oceanographers buzzing around. The chefs are whipping up delicious Chinese cuisine in their kitchen, and the smell of Chinese food is heavenly. The feeling is almost like walking through any Chinatown in the world—San Francisco, Vancouver, Calcutta, or Jakarta. And as in most countries I have visited, I realize there is now a Chinatown in Antarctica and soon it will be mentioned in Lonely Planet.

The Russian base is dominated by a Russian Orthodox Church on top of a hill overlooking the entire cluster of research stations on King George Island. It comes complete with a Russian Orthodox priest brought in from Russia. A tiny but magnificent structure, it is made entirely of logs of wood, with no nails used in its construction, and anchored by chains that rise to the roof to keep it stable in the fierce Antarctic winds that could blow it away like a paper bag. I don't think of Russians at large as particularly religious people; this is more what I would expect from a group of devout Ecuadorean Catholic immigrants in California or Hindu migrant workers from Varanasi brought to Fiji by the British. A group of rational Russian scientists wanting their own church in a remote research station is an unexpected twist—and a startling example of how the human spirit has taken root in this frozen ground.

When our small plane lurches off the gravel runway in wet, windy, squally Antarctic weather, Alejo stands by himself along the runway and waves good-bye in an exaggerated overhead gesture. The sky is gray and cold. The sea looks angry. Alejo cuts a lonely pioneer figure. While we go back to the comforts of the world we know, he stands perfectly happy and at home, trusting himself to one of the most unwelcoming landscapes on the planet. Even this bleak terrain, I have now seen, can support warmth and life—both penguin and human—as well as peaceful cooperation and coexistence and an unearthly beauty of its own. The fact that this vast continent, a frozen desert for the past 23 million years of its 4.5-billion-year existence, has sustained itself, and continues to sustain itself, fills me with a sense of deep and hopeful assurance—a trust that, despite us, our planet and our universe will heal and go on.

CONNECTING THE DOTS AND GETTING OUT OF THE WAY

It all started with Marianne Williamson. Even more correctly, it all started with my dear friend Amandine Roche. It ended with His Holiness the Dalai Lama, Archbishop Desmond Tutu, Reverend Mpho Tutu, Mary Robinson (the first female Irish president), and Sir Richard Branson coming together in a digital eulogy for Nelson Mandela using Google Hangouts. It was one of the proudest moments of my Google career. But at the beginning I could not have connected the dots.

And as is the custom, let us begin at the beginning.

In May 2013, Marianne Williamson was speaking at Google, and I was hosting her. My friend Amandine Roche, visiting from her work with the UN in Afghanistan and Nepal, was attending as my guest. After the talk, as we were standing in the lobby, I pointed out to Marianne the poster that announced her speech and the other speakers at Google that week. Amandine, who was watching from behind us, suddenly squealed in delight, "Oh my God, Dawn Engle and Ivan Suvanjieff of PeaceJam are speaking? I am coming back to hear them. They saved my life once."

She explained that by joining them at their invitation for a meeting with the Dalai Lama in Dharamsala, she had avoided being in Afghanistan on a fateful day when a bomb killed several of her colleagues.

And that is how I met Dawn and Ivan for lunch—because Amandine came back the next day to Google and had lunch with them before their talk. Dawn and Ivan, a former rock star, are a force of nature. They have been nominated for the Nobel Peace Prize a staggering nine times, and their board has 11 Nobel laureates, including the Dalai Lama and Archbishop Tutu.

Fast-forward to December 2013, when Dawn e-mailed me saying that she had recently been in Dharamsala and spoken to Don Eisenberg, who handles digital affairs for the Dalai Lama. I had worked with Don on an earlier program where we featured the Dalai Lama—the Hangout you read about in the chapter "Knock on the Door." Now he was interested in the idea of His Holiness participating in another conversation, and Dawn wanted to meet with me at Google to discuss it. Knocked out by a cold, I told her that I was heading home early and would not be able to meet. This was on Thursday, December 5. Hours later I learned that Nelson Mandela had passed away.

The next day I was in bed nursing my cold when my colleague Ria Tobaccowalah pinged me. She asked if I could help pull together a digital tribute to honor Nelson Mandela's legacy, with the Dalai Lama and Desmond Tutu sharing their memories. At Google the operating philosophy is to work not on incremental ideas, but on ambitious 10X ideas. So even though I had very little sense of how exactly we could make this happen, I told Ria yes and said I would discuss it with Dawn. Dawn told me to put together a proposal and get it in front of the Dalai Lama and the archbishop through their offices.

The day after that, Saturday, was the Google holiday party. My cold felt worse and I felt even more terrible to call my date, Regina, and tell her I would not be able to take her to the party, which she'd been very much looking forward to as a soon-to-be Googler.

Sitting at home in warm clothes and fuzzy bedroom slippers on a cold day in San Francisco and downing large quantities of Yogi Tea, I banged out a proposal. We wanted His Holiness the Dalai Lama and Archbishop Desmond Tutu to remember Nelson Mandela's legacy in a Google Hangout. Anyone in the world would be able to participate by submitting questions through social media. The other leaders I suggested we invite were Jimmy Carter or Bill Clinton, along with Tushar Gandhi, great-grandson of Mahatma Gandhi and head of the Gandhi Foundation. We would also include some schoolchildren from South Africa, Afghanistan, Tibet, and the United States to join the conversation, representing the future of Mandela's legacy. It would be moderated by Nicholas Kristof of *The New York Times*.

I called Don Eisenberg on his cell phone while he was waiting in the New Delhi airport to board a plane to Dharamsala. Don has always been gracious in listening to these wild ideas of mine. He was supportive and said that he would speak the next morning to Tenzin Takhla, the Dalai Lama's chief of staff. He was confident he could convince everyone, especially if Desmond Tutu was participating.

After checking the time in South Africa—too early still—I waited a few hours, drawing the blankets around me, turning the thermostat up, and downing more gallons of herbal tea. I called my colleague Jon Ratcliffe in Johannesburg early Sunday morning just as he was waking up. Jon had been a rainmaker in the past for me, especially on crazy, impossible projects that somehow involved the Dalai Lama and Desmond Tutu. He promised to present the proposal to Benny, who manages Tutu's press affairs, but he also level-set my expectations, reminding me that this was probably the most important week in Benny's entire career as the whole nation was in mourning and preparing for Mandela's funeral. I then sent the proposal to Dawn Engle in Boulder, Colorado. She sent it directly to Tenzin Takhla in Dharamsala and to Desmond Tutu himself to reinforce the request.

In circumstances like these, all you can do is let go and trust that everything happens for a reason. If I had been feeling well, I would have gone to the holiday party with Regina. I would have worked on the proposal on Sunday, and eventually it would have gotten to Desmond Tutu late on Monday. And it is very likely that he would not have seen it and this event would never have happened. Because on Monday Archbishop Tutu was in the midst of preparations to speak at Mandela's memorial service on Tuesday, which was to be the largest gathering of heads of state in history.

I woke up late Sunday morning, checked my e-mail, and rubbed my eyes in disbelief. Tutu had personally responded to Dawn from his iPad, saying he was attracted to the idea but would leave it to his staff to determine if it was possible to schedule it. Don from the Dalai Lama's office had responded too. He had spoken to Tenzin Takhla, and if we could confirm with Desmond Tutu, they would figure out a way to make it work on the Dalai Lama's schedule.

We could not plan much of the logistics till we knew if Archbishop Tutu could participate and from where. We could not reach out to any of the others either till we had the details confirmed. Nicholas Kristof was interested, but he was going to be at a remote location in Kenya with little Internet access.

The team waited with bated breath on Monday, but we got no news. Tuesday brought no news either, which was expected. The attention of the world was riveted on images pouring out of a soccer stadium in Johannesburg, the First National Bank Stadium, where tens of thousands of people gathered—as many as 80,000, by some reports—and leaders from President Zuma to President Obama paid tribute to the greatest son of South Africa.

At midnight Tuesday I boarded a 16-hour flight to Hong Kong. I would be traveling 36 hours door-to-door via Hong Kong, Singapore, and Kochi before I reached my parents' house in Thrissur, India, on my birthday. When we landed in Hong Kong, early Thursday morning local time, I checked my e-mail. Again disbelief. While I was in midflight somewhere over the Pacific Ocean, Desmond Tutu had responded from his iPad. His e-mail read:

> Thx. This old man can do it tomorrow at 4 pm in his office in Milnerton. My home wd not do. No internet line. It is my monthly retreat Friday but I will break my airline 4 this.
>
> Luv
>
> Arch

I wasn't sure what "break my airline" meant—maybe the autocorrect, that constant hazard of typing on a small device, had changed what he was trying to write. But he had signed off saying "Luv, Arch"! The humility of the man was astonishing—responding directly to our e-mails in the midst of one of the busiest weeks of his life, and also an emotionally demanding one, shortly after delivering a moving tribute to his dear friend.

The time when both Tutu and the Dalai Lama could do the Hangout was going to be Friday, December 13, at 4:30 P.M. Cape Town time. That was just 43 hours away. This was where trusting and surrendering became even more effective. I was still in transit and had limited windows of time in the Hong Kong and Singapore airports when I was not in the air. First the boarding area at my gate in Hong Kong, then the Starbucks at Changi Airport in Singapore, became my command center as I launched into calls and e-mails with Dawn in Boulder, Ria in New York, Don in Dharamsala, and Jon in Johannesburg.

Despite the pressure of the time frame, I was cool, calm, and collected. I was confident that they would keep the moving parts going. Nothing motivates my colleagues more than tackling hugely ambitious projects with impossible deadlines and making technology a force for greater good in the world. Googlers rapidly mobilized themselves across four continents, and things started falling into place. All I had to do was get out of the way.

The Dalai Lama was going to be at the Tibetan Youth Hostel in New Delhi, and Don was concerned about the bad Internet connection. No problem. My colleagues in Delhi got a satellite truck to the venue. We needed an anchor, since Nicholas Kristof could not do it from where he was. My colleague Olivia Ma worked her magic in New York and got Anderson Cooper, star anchor at CNN, to come to the Google New York office at 6:30 A.M. on a cold wintry morning. Jon Ratcliffe was on location at Tutu's office testing out the infrastructure. The speed of it all was astonishing. I call it nimbleocity.

On midnight Thursday I arrived at my parents' home in Thrissur, chatted with them briefly, then excused myself and went upstairs to continue working with the rest of the team across the world. Ria told me that we had not heard back yet from the other world leaders we had reached out to, and we still wanted more people to participate to get a diverse expression of tributes to Mandela. I suggested that we should ask Sir Richard Branson or Bono, from the band U2, to join. She agreed that would be fantastic.

Over the years at Google I have learned that when you propose these ideas you are taken seriously because everyone operates with a belief system of expanded possibilities. Jon Ratcliffe put it to me this way in an e-mail when it was all over: "I believe there are big events in one's life which frame the scale of one's thinking." When we succeed at something huge, it changes the scale of the ideas we think are achievable. And we are not limited by not knowing how we're going to accomplish them.

So when Ria replied yes, she seriously meant yes. Except that I had no relationship with Richard Branson or Bono or even any ability to connect with their offices. Unfazed, I checked the time in South Africa—around 10 P.M.—and noticed that Jon Ratcliffe was online. I initiated a Hangout chat and asked him to join, which he did from his bed, using his smartphone. But his camera was turned off. I asked him to turn it on. He did so sheepishly; he was getting ready to go to sleep, and his hair looked all spiky, like a porcupine. I said I didn't care. I wanted to look him in the eye when I made the request.

"Jon, I need a favor from you before you go to bed."

"Tell me, Gopi."

"You worked with Sir Richard Branson and his office recently to do a big program on entrepreneurship on Google+? The one with Elon Musk?"

"Yes, I did, and I built up a good relationship."

"Please reach out to his assistant and tell her we would like Sir Richard to join the conversation and pay his tributes to Mandela."

"I will do my best."

"And, Jon, one more thing. When you are at the archbishop's office tomorrow for testing, please ask Benny or the Arch to reach out to Bono and see if he can join as well."

Then I went back to letting go.

Less than 20 minutes had passed when Jon came back online and sent me a message. "Gopi, Sir Richard's assistant got back to me right away. He will join the conversation. He is flying into London just two hours before the event, so he will join from a lounge in the airport. And he is very comfortable with the technology, so he does not need any extra support or testing from our side." Brilliant. The miracles continued to unfold. A couple of hours later, Ria told me that one of our colleagues had arranged for Mary Robinson to join us as well. In addition to being the first female president of Ireland, Mary is a member of the Council of Elders, the group of "independent global thinkers" that Nelson Mandela had formed, dedicated to peace and human rights.

By now it was 5:30 A.M. on Friday in India. The last time I had lain down on a bed was Tuesday morning, California time. That was 55 hours ago, and jet lag was hitting me. Leaving my colleagues to work on their pieces of the puzzle, I napped for a few hours.

When I got up, there were six hours to go before the start to the event and Amandine was calling me from Kathmandu. Through Dawn's outreach we had a stream of video questions sent in from youth in the United States and South Africa. Amandine was trying to get more questions from students at the Torch of Light School, which belongs to her Amanuddin Foundation in Afghanistan in Kabul, which she had founded while working for the UN in Afghanistan. Now dispatched to Nepal to help monitor the elections there, she was trying to orchestrate it remotely. Unfortunately it was Friday, the Islamic holy day. The supervisor of the school said he could not ask the students to come in, so he would gather some of them in his house and film their questions about the legacy of Nelson Mandela in Afghanistan. The AP cameraman in Kabul wanted to charge a huge amount. Amandine found another cameraman willing to help who gathered his gear and rode a motorbike to show up at the supervisor's door. He filmed the kids asking questions, uploaded the video to YouTube, then sent the link to Amandine in Nepal, where she lives. Amandine then sent the YouTube link to me in India, and, with about two hours to go, I sent it to Olivia Ma at Google so she could send it to Anderson Cooper at CNN in New York. This is the power of technology—to spread wisdom throughout the world.

The dots were connecting. But I could not have seen how that would happen until this very moment. Steve Jobs once said, "You can't connect the dots looking forward; you can only connect them looking backward. So you have to trust that the dots will somehow connect in your future."

At 6:30 P.M. India time, I gathered my parents and sister in the living room in Thrissur to watch the digital tribute. The Dalai Lama gave his trademark giggle and settled down into a chair at the Tibetan Youth Hostel in New Delhi. Archbishop Desmond Tutu and his daughter Reverend Mpho Tutu signed in from their office in Cape Town. Anderson Cooper started making the introductions in his trademark booming voice from New York. And a few minutes later, Sir Richard Branson joined in from London and Mary Robinson from New York. The magic was happening. Their laughter was contagious as these friends reminisced about their long association with Nelson Mandela. We could feel Mandela smiling and waving as well.

Midway through, Anderson Cooper asked the Dalai Lama a question that Qasawallah, an 11-year-old from the Torch of Light School in Kabul, had sent in: "How can we keep Mandela's spirit alive in Afghanistan?"

The Dalai Lama scratched his chin and said, "When you look across history, when human beings encounter difficulties—on a personal or national level—most use force, with counterproductive results. The long-lasting solution is to compassionately approach difficulties, to conquer the mind, and remove hatred. Via this approach, hatred will eventually become love. Now is the time to think about the value of nonviolence in general and the value of forgiveness in particular—in that way, you can build a new atmosphere and counteract this negative feeling of revenge."

In an almost mystical and improbable way, the dots were connecting. Mandela, who had died at 95, was passing his famous Freedom Torch, his own torch of light, through the hands of the 78-year-old Dalai Lama to 11-year-old Qasawallah in Afghanistan, a boy less than half the age the Dalai Lama had been when he'd fled Tibet into exile.

CLIMBING BLIND

I am standing in the Colorado Rockies, looking up. About 40 feet above the ground is a small maze of pathways designed for monkeys, not humans. Tightropes, swings, narrow logs, rope bridges, and dangling knots are anchored to the trees all around. In just a few minutes I am supposed to be traversing this unsteady pathway in the sky.

Standing around me is an assortment of people from all over the United States. Among them are a police officer from New York and a biomedical entrepreneur from Minnesota; a financial planner from Virginia Beach and a third-grade teacher from Austin; a retail store manager with Warner Bros. in Denver and a Harvard Business School grad who runs a $30 million cosmetics line for Lord & Taylor.

For the next several days I will be spending my time with these people in rough, physically challenging outdoor situations in a life and career renewal program for young adults. The program is designed by Outward Bound, which since 1941 has been using wilderness settings both as a classroom and as a metaphor to explore one's understanding of oneself. You are put in a demanding wilderness situation far outside your comfort zone. By stretching physically, mentally, emotionally, and spiritually, you foster a sense of self-worth and an appreciation of human interdependence. The aim is not to break your spirit, but to expand it.

Kim, one of our instructors, advises us on how to deal with the challenge of the ropes course. A third-generation Japanese American, Pilates instructor, and decade-long Outward Bound veteran, she has the gentleness and persuasion of a mother taking her frightened child on his first visit to a petting zoo. "Take some risks," she urges us. "Cross the walkway without holding on to anything, or push yourself and try it blind." She continues encouragingly, "And if you fall, don't worry, your safety harness will prevent you from crashing to the ground." The prospect of dangling from trees high above the ground on a rope and being hauled up by strangers sounds interesting but highly avoidable to me. Alana, who works for the federal government in Washington, has a haunted look on her face. She has told me that she has a fear of heights and that this is her worst nightmare. She decides to stare that fear in the face. She wants to go first.

At one point the maze in the sky forks into two. Turn right and you have to walk a 60-foot tightrope suspended high above a raging river. Turn left and you walk on a narrow log that ends abruptly. At that point you leap across a gap and hope you will land on a narrow shelf on the tree across. This is called the leap of faith. I turn right to take the tightrope across the river. Tracy, the schoolteacher, opts for the leap of faith. She barely catches the shelf and dangles from it with her legs flailing. I am too frightened to look and start gingerly across the tightrope. I try not to pay attention to the raging waters below.

The next day is rock-climbing day. Wolf, the course director, is teaching us new rope tricks. When they named him they must have known that he was born to live in the wilderness. His life is wrapped around mountains, rivers, and the outdoors. He has that weather-beaten look of someone who has seen dozens of seasons change at close quarters. "There are dragons around you," he warns us, holding up a mock Tyrannosaurus rex. "They may not look like what you expect. But there are dragons on these rock faces, and there are dragons within you. Today you have to slay them when you climb these peaks."

We are standing at the bottom of a sheer wall of rock that rises straight up about 100 feet. All day long we will be climbing this wall, ringing a bell at the top, and climbing down. Safety ropes are attached to harnesses around our waists, and we shall be belayed by people whom we met less than a day ago. In Brent, Rosalee, and Jeff we trust. Wolf tells us that once we understand the worst that's likely to happen if we screw up, we are able to deal with our fears. In this case the worst is letting go of your hold completely, dangling from your safety rope, and turning over your life to the belayer below you.

I try this on my first climb. I dangle upside down high on the rock face. The wildflowers that have overgrown the former military camp in the valley below look beautiful upside down. I feel as comfortable as an eagle in the sky. I decide to push myself. I press against the sheer cliff with my hands and legs and go into the yoga pose of Chakrasan (Wheel). My course-mates applaud enthusiastically. I can hear the delighted cry of a personal trainer from New York, "Go, yoga boy!"

I talk with Rosalee in between climbs. She is a tax consultant from St. Louis. I tell her about the remarkable feat of Erik Weihenmayer, a 33-year-old man from Golden, Colorado, not far from where we are standing. Blind since the age of 13, he climbed Mount Everest the previous month, proving from the top of the world that there are no limits to what human beings can achieve. Paul, our climbing instructor, overhears our conversation and asks me if I want to try climbing blindfolded. I think he is joking, but, no, he is serious.

I hesitate, but Paul is gently encouraging. I tie my bandanna around my eyes, check my safety ropes, and start climbing. I find myself using my fingers and sense of touch in ways I had not expected, feeling and testing crevices and holds. I would have thought that taking away one of my most important resources, my eyesight, would keep me from reaching the top. But here I am, using my remaining resources in untapped new ways.

It dawns on me that this is how we go through life: underutilizing our own resources, just like our fine sense of touch that we don't use fully when we climb. It's only when something forces us to dig deeper, when the usual tools don't work, that we realize all the energy and skill and capability we really have at our disposal and see what a difference these resources make. How often do we go through our days—through our *lives*—not living at our peak potential?

And how often do we keep ourselves within what we think are our limits—until we see someone else doing the impossible? After I come down, Paul, our instructor, tries the blindfolded climb himself. He is lyrical in his moves. When he is done, he tells me that this is the first time he has attempted this in his 20-year career. Now there is a long line of people waiting to try rock climbing with a blindfold. Climbing blind was a nutty idea, until I tried it. All of a sudden the possibilities changed and everyone's limitations got redefined.

At the end of the day, I want to try the hardest face of the rock, a section called the Pink Lady. For thousands of years melting snow has ground down this section, polishing away the rock and exposing the pink underbelly. Stephanie, the financial planner, has climbed this face several times already along different routes. "Halfway up, move toward the left," she tells me. "It starts to smoothen at this point and you have to press with your feet to get a little grip. In the last section it's so smooth that there is no traction. Just use your faith and stick to the rock." With those words of wisdom, I start up the Pink Lady.

Halfway to the top, I rest on a ledge and catch my breath. An incredible scene is unfolding to my left. Leigh, the retail store manager from Denver, is starting her climb. She is at a turning point in her life personally and professionally and has been very reflective on the course. When I asked her if she wanted to try the Pink Lady with me, she was hesitant and unsure. When I started my climb she was still hesitating at the base with the rest of the group, not quite committed to attempting it. But she must have found some inner resolve. As I stop to take a deep breath, I look down to see that Leigh is attempting to climb blindfolded.

A hush descends over the group. Leigh goes through her routine and starts the safety checks with her belay partner. "Check harness . . . Harness ready . . . Ready to climb . . . Up rope. . . Climbing." Like a spider she spreads her hands and legs on the rock. Her sensorial antennae tell her about cracks, crevices, ridges, knobs, and shelves. Toward the top she is so tired that she is able to use only her hands to lift herself. She takes about four times the normal climbing time to finish. Back on the ground, when she takes her blindfold off, I can see new energy in her eyes. In her quiet way she does not brag about it or thump her chest. But I can tell that a dam has broken inside her heart.

GETTING TO THE NEXT RIDGE

Day three of my Outward Bound adventure. We are rafting the Browns Canyon stretch of the Arkansas River. The river guides and our instructors are bantering while I focus on not falling out of the raft. I hear snatches of the conversation. "Yesterday it was 2300, today it is down to 2100." I am dismayed. "Wow, has the Nasdaq dropped that low?" I ask. With disbelief in the narrowness of the world I occupy, they tell me that they are discussing the water discharge in the river.

The instructors share a deep reverence for the surroundings that I find moving. "Don't fight the river," Samantha the river guide tells us. "The river will always win. Just go with the flow, literally." Wolf, the course director, puts it another way: "Mountains don't know that they are 13,000 feet or 20,000 feet. They will present you with the same level of challenge and love. Respect the mountain and you will enjoy the climb."

We make camp in a meadow by a river, our base before we attempt to climb Galena Mountain, a 13,000-foot peak in the Sawatch Range. Paul, one of the instructors who will climb with us—who most of the year is an English professor at the University of Colorado, fond of reciting poetry by Mary Oliver and arguing about Oscar Wilde—asks us if we want to climb the peak under the full moon and spend the night on top. Most of the team jumps up enthusiastically. I want to do it too, but I am just a little nervous. I realize we will be changing the rules. We will be climbing without the benefit of a night's rest. Markedly, the visibility will be much worse than during the day, a distinct disadvantage in unfamiliar terrain. And we will have to carry extra weight up the mountain in order to spend the night on the top. But I decide to go along and test how much I can stretch physically and mentally.

Paul picks out a game trail and asks me, as the slowest plodder, to lead the group up the mountain. I am not very athletic and do not hike up mountain trails well. If I had been born 100 years ago, I would probably have been eaten by a tiger in the jungles of my native India when I failed to outrun it. All the same, I set out eagerly.

Within an hour I feel exhausted. The path is steep. The thin air at this elevation makes us pant at every step. The moon is yet to come up, and climbing with a coal miner's headlamp somehow seems more tiring. My back is killing me, and I deeply regret the useless things I added to my backpack. What was I really thinking when I threw in my electric razor?

Now the mountain starts playing tricks on us. We spot a ridge that looks to be just 20 minutes away and then a short walk to the peak. When we get to the ridge there is another one just beyond it. There turn out to be dozens of ridges in an unending chain. Slowly, the enthusiastic conversation dies out as the group falls prey to fatigue. As I look around, all I see is a long line of silent human beings shuffling up the mountain. No voices, just the rustle of outdoor gear, some hard breathing, an occasional sigh. Too tired to talk, too far from the peak to see the whole route clearly, all we can do is focus on getting to the next ridge.

Twice in recent years I have been in between jobs. The last time it happened, I decided to take time off to reflect on the next phase of my professional passions, as I call it. I spent five months traveling to nine countries, from Iceland to India to Bahrain to Zambia, and climbing Kilimanjaro. During this time, I asked myself questions such as "What does the next step of my career look like? What do I truly value?" And then while on a retreat at my guru Rama Devi's center in Shakthinagar, Mangalore, India, I clarified and wrote down what I valued most in work and life. Then, using this list, I asked myself, "What companies most reflect these values?" I came up with three names, and Google was at the top of the list. When I came back to Silicon Valley, I was absolutely clear and focused on where I wanted to work. I entered into discussions with all three companies and received offers from two. A few months later I joined Google and have not looked back since.

During that transition, I could not imagine the role I am in now. I couldn't see the ultimate destination. However, I could see the next step—the next ridge. Once I got there, I could see the next step, then the one after, and so forth, each step leading to the next until I got where I wanted to go.

Here on Galena, wild game take the easiest path up the mountain, and following them is our best bet. But in the darkness we cannot find the trail and perversely we seem to be taking the hardest route. We bushwhack our way through willows as they cling to our packs and hold us back, then suddenly we are sinking knee deep into soft snow. As we change direction to get out of the snow, we find ourselves in a field of talus climbing over big boulders, some of them snow covered, some of them rocking alarmingly.

I think of the San Diego Marathon I ran two years ago. I was completely spent by mile 21. Mentally I was prepared to finish, but my body had given up its last ounce of energy and abandoned the course. My spirit was willing, but the flesh had fled. I had to reach out to the psychic energy of the other runners, the cheering crowds, and the rock bands playing at every mile. It was the hardest physical challenge I had ever accomplished. This feels twice as hard, and the next ridge seems impossibly far away.

So I reach out yet again to the others. They offer a mystic embrace. I plug in to the group's energy, and they give liberally. Mike, a mortgage broker from Chicago, walks behind me constantly, and his encouragement somehow seems to be propping me up. He is turning over his amazing reserves to me. I simply accept whatever support anyone gives.

I am concerned about Judy, just out of the Ph.D. program at the University of Illinois, scheduled to start work at the Centers for Disease Control in Atlanta after the course is done. She has kept a sense of calm and control through the week so far. But now it is obvious that she is way past her limit. She has a night vision problem and climbing in the moonlight is especially challenging. Occasionally she stumbles and stops. Her look says, *I know I can't take the next step, but somehow I will.*

I have no idea what time of the night it is and where on the mountain we are. I have no idea how far we have to climb. But one thing we do know: for the first time on the climb we are standing in a spot on the mountain that is dry and flat, that allows us to lie down without sliding to the bottom of the mountain in our sleeping bags. This is where we will spend the rest of the night.

As the sun comes up in the morning, we stir and look around. The summit is in view, closer than I expected—it looms practically right above us. With a final burst of energy, we reach it as a team. The view is majestic in every direction. Peaks with names like the Castle and the Belles surround us, and shiny, glistening lakes shimmer in the distance. What we see in front of us is at once enormous and overpowering. As Maria, the executive from New York, tells me later, "Only eagles can comprehend the world in such perspective."

The climb has been an emotional experience. I am so overwhelmed that I embrace the summit rock and kiss it. Lisette, the personal trainer, asks if we can all be silent for a few minutes. She gazes at the lakes in the distance and simply weeps. I look on in amazement and wonder how much richer my life would be if I lived it with the same level of emotion she does.

Sitting on the peak, our instructor Kim asks me to read aloud a quote that she says is from the explorer and journalist Walter Bonatti: "We [climbers] demonstrate in the most stunning way of all—at the risk of our lives—that there is no limit to the effort man can demand of himself. This quality is the basis of all human achievement. . . . We prove that there is no limit to what man can do."

EXPAND,
DON'T BREAK

The crowning glory of every Outward Bound program is the wilderness solo, when you spend time in the outdoors all by yourself with no human contact. The experience is based on the African tradition of sending young men into the wilderness to survive on their own in the bush. It is a rite of passage.

As the sun begins to set, our guides Paul and Kim brief us on the wilderness solo and advise us to find a place in the forest that feels special and spiritual to us. They also tell us how to be safe during the solo and remind us to purify the water from the stream before drinking it.

Charlene, a young mother from New York, wants to know what happens if we see a bear. Paul reassures us that it would be a real blessing without much real danger. "The bear will say, 'Oh, humans,' and charge in one direction, and you are going to say, 'Oh, a bear,' and charge in the other direction." This description of bear–human wilderness protocol does not necessarily make us any braver, but we set off in search of our versions of Walden Pond. Fittingly, one of the items in my backpack is Henry David Thoreau's description of his own more extensive wilderness solo.

I find a clearing that feels suitably sacred to me. It is in the middle of a large open meadow, in a valley surrounded by snow-covered peaks. A river runs through the middle. A cluster of pine trees in a perfect circle acts as a great windbreak. I pitch my tent in this cluster and make it my new home. Through a gap in the trees I can look across the meadow at a tall and majestic mountaintop.

The minimalism is stark but liberating. It is just me, my thoughts, my books, and the constant presence of wilderness around. I recall my ethics professor, Tom Donaldson, at business school at Wharton leaving us with a quote during the last class. It was by the Jewish philosopher Rabbi Balfour Brickner: "It is what we do when we are alone, no one is looking, and we know we won't be caught, that makes all the difference between a civilization and a jungle." Last night around the campfire, Lisette and Charlene had jokingly threatened to do naked solos. But in a metaphorical sense they may have been right. In a wilderness solo you are indeed naked. What you think and do is between you and the wind.

This wilderness solo I am doing lasts 24 hours. As I settle in to sleep for the night under the open sky, I become aware that I am not alone in my large bedroom under the stars. I have company, from a colony of ants to mocking owls to creatures of the night that my mind manufactures at a furious pace with every moving branch and every rustling leaf.

In the morning as the sun comes up, I embark on the formal exercise of writing down what I feel my life should be about. The principles I had developed during my retreat at the New Camaldoli hermitage are even clearer in my mind. But what dawns on me now, what excites me about dedicating myself to my principles, is the true import of the phrase "What doesn't kill you strengthens you." In the last week, I came up against physical and mental limitations. And each time, I broke through to a new level of possibility. But more than what I achieved was this sense I gained of what was possible.

When Kim comes to pick me up and take me back to base camp, she looks at me with a knowing smile. I take this to mean that every time she comes up to get someone from the mountains after a wilderness solo, they have the mad but serene look of a sage who has just had an epiphany.

All philosophers, in one way or another, embark on this exercise of going off into the wilderness—into the depth of solitude that wisdom springs from. For our group, it is an opportunity to pay a deeper kind of attention to things we don't normally see. At home, we have television; on solo, we watch wildlife go by. We can live on much less—and with much less "stuff"—than we imagine. And it's interesting, as the rabbi said, to see what we do, what choices we make, when no one is watching.

Gathered around a flickering campfire on the first night we are back together again, we talk about our solo experiences. Some people were perfectly happy and self-contained during their time apart. They dipped into an inner life that stimulated and sustained them. Craig, an industrial engineer from Arkansas, spent a good portion of his time thinking about his autistic son, Michael, who has taught his family profound lessons. For him and his wife, raising Michael—and letting go of any expectations of how parenthood, or their child, "should" be—has meant finding new dimensions of selfless and unconditional love. His touching account moves everyone deeply.

Others were driven crazy by the loneliness and perceived lack of stimulation. They realized how much they had surrounded themselves with the noise of modern life, the way we are surrounded by the air we breathe. Brett in particular described how unnerving he found it to spend the night alone. Normally he would be surrounded by kids and an extended family. There would also be TV, music, and all the distractions that come packaged with a blessed American life. Bereft of all that, he realized that there was an empty hole in his life that he did not know existed. In the deafening silence, he was so overwhelmed that he just broke down and cried. A big bear of a man, sitting on a rock in the wilderness and crying.

This is what happens when you go into nature and into solitude. Either you tap into a rich inner life, comfortable in your own skin and your own company, or you discover a void that you've been using artificial stimulation to cover up—and that, if you want to, you can start to find a new way to fill.

For me, the Outward Bound course has been intense and transformational, and despite the physical challenges that facilitated this transformation, I am still in one piece! Lisette calls it a sacred experience that will be just between the mountains and us.

In the cauldron that the Outward Bound program provided, we all looked at our lives colored by our own experiences. The solo gave us space to begin to deconstruct it. It started us on an unhurried journey of deconstructing and reflecting that, we hope, will bring us to a wise new understanding of our life in its context—what the Buddha called the *suchness* or the *is-ness* of each of our lives.

HOPE IN AN OLD NEWSPAPER

It's Friday evening in Hong Kong. Two years into my first real job, a software programmer for a supermarket chain. As I do every week, I've hopped the train for the one-hour ride from my apartment to the main ferry pier at Victoria Harbour, once the gateway for the British to the magical kingdom of China and epicenter of the opium trade, now a major port for exporting goods from China to the rest of the world. Tonight, out on the wind-whipped water, huge freighters crawl to and from the open waters of the China Sea, leisure crafts and water taxis zip in and out of harbor traffic, ferries loaded with passengers chug across the channel to Kowloon. Constant movement. Constant noise. Street traffic, boat engines, and the distinct sound unique to Hong Kong, the sound of money being made.

On Man Yu Street, hawkers call from their make-shift stands, pushing cheap toys, bad plastic flowers, fake watches—Rolex, Cartier, and Tourbillon. Cooks fry, sear, and steam. As I approach the stalls, it's as though I pass through some olfactory territorial boundary. I move from zone to zone, the pungent aroma of the bean-curd cart mutating into the uncomfortably nasty odor from the fried-chicken-feet cart blending with the strange smells from the cart with unrecognized foods that makes me quicken my pace.

I move on to the stalls featuring three-day-old newspapers that passengers on international flights have left on the plane, and that, from what I gather, the cleaning crew sells to the hawkers. You can't buy English-language newspapers from other cities—not in newsstands or bookstores. To the tiny expat population, hungry for any kind of news from back home or from the rest of the world, these hawkers provide the only opening for information.

So every week, on Friday or Saturday, I buy newspapers lifted from the Cathay Pacific flight from San Francisco to Hong Kong, the *San Francisco Chronicle* and the *San Jose Mercury News*, papers the guide books promote as the top in the Bay Area, papers I read for hours, poring over job listings. These out-of-date papers, wrinkled, stained with coffee, tea, overcooked airplane food, represent a window to a whole other, shinier world I have only read about, heard about, and seen in movies. I'm excited, hungry to travel, to live in yet another country. These papers are my gateway, the gold mine of information I need to meet my goal—find a job in the United States, specifically the San Francisco Bay Area.

When I reach my favorite news stall, I reach into my wallet for the Hong Kong dollar I need. The bill lies next to a newspaper clipping I found in *The South China Post,* an ad for an American company. The ad boasts an American flag. I carry the clipping because a few months earlier, my boss told me about his goal-setting strategy, about how when he took guitar lessons, he carried a guitar plectrum in his pocket to remind him to practice every day. Every time he reached in his pocket he was reminded of his goal. So I keep my ad with the American flag with me always.

I remember picking the Bay Area simply because a classmate of mine from grad school was working on his Ph.D. at the University of California–Berkeley. Plus it was, and still is, the technology capital of the world. I wanted to quit my job straight away and move there, take my chances, but since I had three weeks of vacation coming, I decided to take a pilot trip to check out my options. I polished my résumé and printed 30 copies to send to companies that were advertising positions. That's how you did it then: printed out copies and sent them through the post.

I didn't want to list a Hong Kong residence on my résumé because companies were hesitant to hire someone from outside the United States—a lot of red tape—so I listed my friend's phone number and address as my own. I FedExed my résumés to him so he could post them locally. I also asked him to change the message on his phone machine to "Hi, you've reached Rakesh and Gopi, we're not here, please leave your message." In my cover letter I said I'd follow up on June 14 (which was when I was coming to the U.S.).

I flew into San Francisco on June 12. Rakesh drove to the airport to meet me, then we rode back to Berkeley. We stopped at the bus stop two blocks from the YMCA, where Rakesh had booked a room for me. "When you want to go to the university and back, you want to take this bus. When you return, you can just walk the two blocks from the bus stop to the Y. But if you come back at night, you get off the bus and you run. Otherwise you will be dead."

Is he serious? I wondered. *Pulling my leg?* I didn't know. When I got to the YMCA, I picked up a local free newspaper and read about a carjacking and a mugging on Allston Way, the very street where the Y was located. I decided to take my friend seriously. The next day, Sunday, I headed out to pick up the newspaper to check out job opportunities. The guy at the YMCA front desk made change for the coin-operated newspaper racks and directed me to the closest news racks on the corner of Allston and Shattuck Avenue. News racks didn't exist in India or Hong Kong, so I set out from the Y trusting I'd know these racks when I saw them.

I walked toward Shattuck, deep in urban America, past people hanging out on the sidewalk. They seemed big, burly, and intimidating, from their street clothes to their demeanor and attitude. Everything seemed larger than I'd imagined—wider streets, bigger cars. Thank God I'd spent some time in Hong Kong, which gave me some familiarity with an intense urban environment. Still, it was an urban area in a new country, and the street scene looked very frightening to me.

I kept on. Acting cool. Like I knew what I was doing. One of the points I'd learned from my guidebook was that you never wanted to look as though you were lost. Don't stand in the dark under a streetlamp with a big city map spread out, looking like you completely do not know where to go. That behavior screams "tourist," a lightning rod for muggers. So I was determined to avoid looking like a tourist. That was my plan to stay safe. Head down. Cool.

When I reached the news rack, I dug in my pocket for the $1.50 I needed to buy a paper. I pulled out change, any change, shoving in coin after coin, dimes, nickels, quarters. (I had no idea the machine accepted only quarters!) I waited. Obviously, nothing happened. I tugged at the handle. The door wouldn't budge. Casually, I pulled again. The news rack spit out all my coins, scattering them all over the sidewalk, where they bounced off the curb, into the gutter. So much for blending in.

"Sir," a man carrying a tub of coins said. "Do you need any help? Do you need some coins?" I think he kept 10 cents on the dollar. At the time, though, I didn't realize making change was his business. *I know how this will work,* I thought. *I'll reach for my wallet to hand over a dollar, and this guy's going to grab my wallet and run.* So I said, "No, thank you," and walked away briskly, trying to look very normal, leaving my coins behind, because I thought picking them off the street would be a dead giveaway.

At the next corner, I tried the same thing, got the same result. No newspaper, coins clanging all over, man with a tub of coins asking if I needed change, me pretending I needed nothing at all. *I'm cool.* I tried again. And again. Finally I headed back to the Y. No paper. All my coins gone. On my way, I passed the guy who worked at the front desk. "How ya doin'?" he asked. I was so thrilled! Where I came from in India, people on the streets didn't really pay that much attention to each other. *Wow,* I thought, *the U.S. is just such a friendly country. Random strangers care about you and they want to know how you're doing.* So I responded, telling him I'd just arrived, how I was still jetlagged, still not used to the place, and then I realized he hadn't even slowed his pace. Here I was, chatting away, and he kept on walking by. *Why did he ask if he didn't want to know?* I wondered. Of course now I know, when someone asks how you're doing, you keep the non-conversation moving by bypassing any reference to your well-being, lobbing the same question right back—*How ya doin'?*—and keep walking.

Before I moved to the U.S. with $7,000 to my name and no job, my family couldn't understand why I would leave my position in Hong Kong for total uncertainty. I worked for a well-run corporation, earning a nice salary.

I should stay there. My dad had worked for one company for 35 years. My family was a very risk-averse, conservative, middle-class family. Once you got a good job, in their view, you never, ever left. You held on to it, because it was so hard to get a job. "What happens if you don't get a job there?" they asked me.

But I wasn't worried. That three-week trip to Berkeley, where I sat every day in the YMCA hallway, dropping coins into the pay phone, calling potential employers, arranging 13 interviews—even landing a few second interviews that I couldn't go to because my vacation was up—gave me the confidence that I could make the move and find a job, that I could work the whole thing out.

That day in June when I arrived at the San Francisco airport for the first time, the airport had overwhelmed me. I'd retrieved my bags and cleared customs, then set off to call my friend, Rakesh, who was waiting for me to call him, so he could pick me up. We had no cell phones then, so I needed to call on a pay phone, but I had no idea how much money to put in. I went to the currency exchange, where they gave me some bills and coins. I showed the man my friend's phone number and asked how many coins I needed.

"A few dimes and nickels will be fine," he told me, handing me a me a fistful of coins. Only when I got to the phone and looked at the coins in my hand, none of the coins had "dime" or "nickel" on them. Instead, every coin read *E Pluribus Unum* (which I later learned translated to "one from many"). Every single coin. The words looked like English to me, but I had no idea what they meant. I flipped one of the coins over, thinking maybe the other side would yield more information, but it just read *In God we trust.*

I stood there, bags at my feet, surrounded by the sound of suitcase wheels on tile, throngs of travelers arriving and departing, laughing with friends and loved ones, or heads down, intent on their destinations. I stood there, in the midst of newsstands peddling miniature cable cars and sourdough bread, rubbing my thumb unconsciously over the thin ridged edge of what I now know is a dime. No idea what to do. I scrutinized the coin again. "In God we trust." *Okay,* I thought, *okay.*

I grabbed my bags and walked out into the San Francisco summer sunshine, rendered cold by the fog rolling in from the Pacific, past the San Andreas Fault on the Pacific Rim at the edge of the entrance to the bay. Rakesh picked me up, and I made it to the Berkeley YMCA. I went to my 13 interviews, flew back to Hong Kong, returned to the U.S., landed a job, shelled out most of my limited savings for a beat-up Honda and a run-down apartment in an East Bay suburb with many other immigrants like me getting started on their new lives, spent every Wednesday night attending Toastmasters meetings at the neighborhood Unity Church to hone my speaking skills . . . in other words, I trusted. I leapt. I landed safely.

PART V

THANK YOU FOR SUBSCRIBING

From her hotel in the middle of war-torn Afghanistan to my condo in Silicon Valley, my friend Amandine and I message our lists of what we're grateful for. Lucking onto the path of yoga and meditation makes our list; so does our health, and so does Google Hangouts, our vehicle for expressing gratitude, in the moment, across more than 7,000 miles.

A few years ago, our exchange would not have been possible. If we take a step back and recall what our lives were like even five years ago, we can't help but wonder at the breathtaking scope and possibilities of how far we've come.

It's amazing, the amount of power and capability that technology has put into our hands—the ability to connect with each other and to access information. For all this information, this massive organization, we can thank the collective—those who continue to develop and maintain the technology. Those who upload the cat video, create the guitar-tuning app, post the politically charged article about debt, and enter the recipe for vegan brownies. Those who simply read articles, eat brownies, or own a cat—all of us. Humanity as a whole. Grateful for what is. Embracing the possible. Engaging. Signing up for life itself.

THE INTERCONNECTION OF ALL HUMAN BEINGS

I am walking along the banks of the Yamuna River in Vrindavan, India. Every *Bhagavad Gita*–quoting pundit-philosopher here is happy to talk to me about the interconnection of all human beings, the oneness of all humanity. This oneness is a core philosophy espoused by Krishna in the *Bhagavad Gita,* and this is where it all originated. Brindavan is the cosmic playground where the blue-skinned, flute-playing, impossibly good-looking Krishna cavorted with his thousand beautiful milkmaid girlfriends—his Gopis—on a scale reserved for the gods.

Now, 5,000 years later, I see how it is all playing out, starting with a modest mobile phone. With my own Android smartphone forgotten in the business center at Dubai International Airport, I decide I need to stay connected even as my assistant is working on retrieving my phone and getting it shipped to me. What if one of the milkmaids, the Gopis, wants to call me? Having been named after Krishna as Gopinath, the Lord of the Gopis, I think it quite possible that the phone may ring. A five-minute transaction in a small store in a bylane next to the iconic Krishna Balaram temple (in a town with 5,000 temples) is all I need to walk out armed with a number and a phone in my hands.

I contemplate the power I am holding. These little things are now the 79th organ in the human body. Of course, it hasn't always been this way. I recall that in my childhood, every summer my parents would ship me off to Chittilamchery so that I could run wild with my cousins and drive my grandparents crazy. Watch the rice grow in my grandfather's waterlogged paddies plowed by water buffaloes. Or join my grandmother as she milked our single cow and then made me drink the fresh milk almost straight from the cow's udder (with a little boiling in between) so that I could be shipped back to my parents with chubbier cheeks. Back then in Chittilamchery, for a village of 20,000 people we had three phones. One in the post office, one in the medical store, one in the school headmaster's office. They had two-digit numbers and an operator manually connected you to the number you wanted by pushing wires into sockets. I considered myself a child prodigy because I carried the whole phone book for the village in my head. I still do—31, 32, and 33.

Today as I return with my parents for a ceremony in the village temple dedicated to the presiding goddess, Cherunatturi Bhagavathy, I notice that everyone walking the small pathways along the rice paddies has a mobile phone. Tucked into little bundles in the folds of their white mundus is an amazing amount of power to manifest human interconnection.

There are an estimated 7 billion–plus mobile cellular connections on the planet. Assume for a minute that each one of them is in the hands of a different member of our human family of 7.2 billion people. Then think about what is now possible: that Velayudhan, walking along the paddy fields, whose father, Ponnuchamy, plowed my grandfather's paddies, can punch in 15 digits and—standing next to Valiya Kandum, the big paddy field in front of our house—have a conversation with any one of his 7-billion-plus brethren. He can capture an image of the buffalo in front of him and send it racing to cousin Krishnan Kutty working in a hotel in Qatar. Geography is not an obstacle anymore. Distance is not a hurdle. Nor is language, because applications like Google Translate can help us translate between language pairs from a choice of 90 languages. Hindi to Hmong, Gujarati to Greek, Tamil to Turkish. So Velayudhan can type in Tamil and have it sent in Russian to Tatyana from Novosibirsk. This is an unprecedented capability of connection that humanity is experiencing. All from the middle of the paddies of Chittilamchery, where six years ago, when I brought my Wharton classmates Hal, Brian, Melissa, and Laura to visit, they were among the first Westerners to set foot here.

Sitting at the airport in Thiruvananthapuram, India, where I studied at the local Government Arts College, I decide to push the boundaries some more. The snack shop also doubles as a gateway to the world. Three Internet-enabled terminals tempt me. Just 100 rupees (US$2) for an hour includes a free cup of masala chai with copious amounts of elaichi, inchi, cloves, and other spices that grow in the fertile, moist hillsides of Kerala. I go to my Google account and invite the world to join me at the Thiruvananthapuram airport in a public Hangout chat on video.

First one to find me is Murino Norinho from São Paulo. He speaks Portuguese. But using Google Translate, we start a merry banter going back and forth between Portuguese and English. Vinil Menon from Kochi, India, joins us, tempted by my name and location. He whooshes in delight when I launch into rapid-fire Malayalam, our mother tongue. Back in San Francisco, Emel Mutlu, one of my very good friends from work, is preparing her four-year-old son, Arda, for bed-time; she notices me hanging out and jumps in with Arda. Emel is Turkish and grew up in a refugee camp in Bulgaria before coming to America; now Arda is gurgling in Turkish to her, delighted by this multimedia sensory experience.

Since it is December, we all decide to don reindeer ant-lers. Why not? Janahan, a brilliant engineer originally from Sri Lanka who sits next to me in the office, created this clever feature for the holiday season. At the click of a but-ton, any of us can put on a virtual reindeer nose and set of antlers, and as we move our heads the antlers stay on our heads on-screen. Janahan had explained to me that this was an extremely hard problem to solve and needed a complex computer-science solution. The software detects the eyes and decides where to place the nose and the antlers. As we move our heads around in real time, it processes the video images and recalculates dynamically where the antlers should show up on the screen. But what gifted engineers like Janahan do is to hide away this complexity so that four-year-olds like Arda can connect effortlessly with other reindeer.

Murino decides that this is too good a party for his four-year-old brother, Carlos, to miss and brings him into the Hangout. Soon Carlos and Arda are pointing to each other in the unself-conscious way kids do. Mysteriously, they can communicate to each other in Turkish and Portuguese and make fun of each other's antlers. This is a delightful play-ground for adults and children halfway across the world. Uniting India, America, Brazil, Turkey. Weaving together En-glish, Malayalam, Turkish, Portuguese in one room.

All of a sudden it dawns on me that this is what they were talking about in Brindavan. That essential truth, that interconnection that all human beings share, is what we are seeing on our screens right now. The oneness of humanity, with reindeer antlers.

My Cup
Runneth Over

Life sometimes hits us like a ton of bricks. And when that happens there is a bigger problem than the bricks now piled on top of us. The problems are those negative stories recurring in our head when our cup which once overflowed is now empty.

Ten years ago, my life felt like a Bollywood movie. I was living in a dream house, enjoying professional success, and my personal life was perfect. Then suddenly things started falling apart. There are six pillars that hold a person's life together—your home, your relationship, your job, your health, your community, and your sense of self. In one week three of these crumbled. I was reminded of a quote that's often attributed to Mother Teresa: "I know God does not give me anything I can't handle. I just wish he didn't trust me so much." In my own situation I felt as if I was being trusted with way more than what I could handle. I lost my job, I lost my house, and I lost my long-term relationship—my life had turned into a country-western song.

Sitting on the edge of my bed, in my quiet and dark bedroom, I refused to face reality. Still, the negative stories replaying in my head haunted me.

I turned on the TV. There at 3 A.M. was motivational speaker Tony Robbins, challenging me: "Live with passion. If you feel your cup is half empty, change your belief to say my cup is half full!" I shot back in frustration, "Tony, you don't understand. *My . . . cup . . . is . . . fully . . . empty.*"

It was then I heard the voice of reason. It was my dad's voice, and he was saying, "Son, when life gives you an empty cup, you are lucky because now you can fill it with your heart's desire."

I spoke to my dear friend Stuart, who also acts as my coach and mentor. He made me answer a question that fundamentally changed the lens through which I was viewing my situation. The question was: "What is the greater good in this situation?"

Instantly, that changed my perspective. Have you ever had one of those moments where things that appeared one way suddenly show themselves in a new light?

The negative stories in my head started changing. Instead of feeling anxious about losing my job, I had a sense of relief, as I could now devote all my time to dealing with my personal situation instead of the demands of my work. Instead of being depressed about not being a homeowner, I felt fortunate that I did not have to worry about mortgage payments in a situation like this.

Though unemployed, I now felt empowered. Wow! I could not believe it. So as a new CUO—Chief Unemployed Officer—I gave myself a six-month vacation. Thanks to the kindness and hospitality of friends around the world, I embarked on a journey of discovery.

One of the blessings in my life has been a large group of friends scattered across the world. There are friends from different contexts: classmates from school or university, colleagues in previous jobs who were also good friends.

I had stayed in touch with them and they were always gracious in inviting me to come visit them when I got a chance. And I would have to say no all the time, mainly because of the time it would take and the limited vacation time I had when working. All of a sudden there was an opportunity blossoming in front of me. Since I was no longer working I could choose to give myself as much time off to travel as I needed. And since I had flexibility and was not traveling in peak vacation season like everyone else, I could pick my date of departure or take advantage of fire-sale prices on the Internet to travel at short notice and thus relatively inexpensively. Add to this the fact that I had received a modest severance package and that many of my travel destinations were inexpensive in terms of cost of living. And all of a sudden a window of exciting travel around the world opened up for me.

I traveled from the cold, desolate glaciers of Iceland to the hot, glitzy desert city of Dubai, then to the majestic plains of Kenya. And to really, really fill my cup to the brim, I climbed the tallest mountain in Africa, Kilimanjaro. Altitude sickness kept me from reaching the top, but I did climb the mountain.

Standing on Kilimanjaro, I looked down on the plains of Africa. I realized that my true journey of discovery was not the one that was taking me around the world but the one that was leading me within. On *that* journey, I was discovering that essential truth: Our life situations are not our real problems. It's those negative stories recurring in our head.

Returning home, I rebuilt my life, not without difficulty. Finding a job with Google and creating a haven in a lovely home on a small island overlooking the water were the first two pillars to be rebuilt after what had crumbled earlier. But the new stories I came back with were even more profound. The life we are living may not be the life we chose. But it is the life we have been given. And we can choose to live it with grace and dignity. Sometimes our lives may feel as though they are spiraling out of our control. But we have a choice in how we respond. And you can choose the responses that let you, years later, tell your friends, "I am proud of the path I took."

I learned many things from my journey. But when I really want to be reminded of the power of our stories, I look to my friend Jason Becker.

At 18, Jason was one of the world's best guitarists. At 19, he was diagnosed with Lou Gehrig's disease, which atrophied all his muscles. Today, at 45, Jason is completely paralyzed and needs a respirator to breathe. When I first met Jason, the story in my head was that "Jason's life is so tragic." A compassionate story, but a negative one—his cup seemed truly empty to me.

The story in Jason's head is radically different.

The disease ruthlessly took away his power of speech. But among the few muscles he could still move were his eyes. Refusing to surrender, he and his father developed a sign language using eye movements. Jason happily calls himself the sexiest man alive and invites us to life's fullness. Recently he released another album of music that he has composed. On one track, you will hear a rhythm loop. *Ha . . . Ha . . . Ha . . . Ha . . .* the sound of Jason breathing through his respirator. Jason has defiantly used the only sound that he can make to continue delighting us with his musical creativity. To me, he is positive proof that our life situations are not our real problems. It's those negative stories recurring in our head when our cup which once overflowed is now empty.

The question is not *if* you will encounter life's challenges. It's *when*. Welcome to this most inclusive club, where all the members have problems, some health, others wealth, and if they are lucky, just relationships. That is the "suchness" of things. It is essential humanity at work.

The only thing I can tell you with certainty is that there will be uncertainty and upheaval in your life. This is how the script of every life runs. How you deal with the full catastrophe of life when it happens is a powerful choice that is available to you. Some people disintegrate. Some people surf the waves.

So what are you going to do when your cup is empty? Fill it, fill it with your heart's desire until your cup once again runneth over.

ATTITUDE OF GRATITUDE

I first met my good friend Amandine Roche at our spiritual teacher's—Amma's—ashram in Amritapuri, in Kerala, India. Now Amandine has traveled from France to the U.S. and is staying with me for an extended visit. She's driving me to work, heading south to the Googleplex on the Silicon Valley artery of Highway 101, keeping pace with the morning traffic—techies, businesspeople, racing to their desks and heavy schedules—when I ask her, "What are you grateful for?" Amandine is used to me blurting out questions like this one. Without missing a beat, she says, "I am grateful that I'm here in San Francisco and sitting in the car right next to you." She glances at me. "What are *you* grateful for?"

For a moment, I'm quiet, considering my answer, and then I say, "I'm grateful for the fact that we lucked our way onto the path of yoga and meditation and want to use it as tools for transforming our respective worlds." (For me, that world is business, for her, war-torn Afghanistan.) We continue taking turns, fueling each other's gratitude until we pull into the parking lot of my building at Google. As I enter the building, I'm in that place of appreciation, that place of *Wow, I am so lucky.* I feel as though I am one of the most blessed people on the planet.

I have to confess, I got the idea of practicing gratitude from self-help author and motivational speaker Tony Robbins. One night at 3 A.M., I was sitting in the living room of my apartment, watching TV infomercials, and there he was again, Tony, the man who had reminded me to see my cup half-full, advertising his 30-day Personal Power program. Personal power sounded good to me, so I picked up the phone, dialed in, and gave the operator "standing by" my credit card number. This was during an era when you picked up a phone, dialed it, and talked to people on the other end instead of ordering milk, taking 33 photos of one person, or tracking every step you take. The fact that the sole purpose of these devices was to use your voice to communicate with another human and there was actually someone on the other end was the most interesting aspect of these phones.

I couldn't wait for the package to arrive in the mail, and when it did, I listened to the course constantly— driving in the car, at home. Everywhere. On one of his modules, Tony suggested taking ten minutes each day to focus on everything you're grateful for.

I gave the exercise a try. I was hooked. And for the past 15 to 20 years, pretty much every day, I've taken five minutes to focus on my gratitude. As I'm cycling to work in the morning, or running, or waiting for a conference call to begin, I try to think of the things I'm grateful for, and if I'm near a pen and paper, I jot them down. I know this exercise might seem simple, trivial, New Agey, or woo-woo, and that's why some people may dismiss it, but it works. Like magic. Once I get started, my brain takes off, churning out the most creative thoughts, both playful and serious, taking me in all kinds of different directions. It's amazing what comes up. On some days, Sundays and Thanksgiving, say, I might list up to 100.

Sometimes people ask me if they need to come up with a list of completely new things every day. Not necessarily. I could build a list of new items every single day for 100 days without duplicating any of them, but I do tend to repeat certain items, such as gratitude for my parents. There's nothing wrong with being even more grateful today for something you were grateful for yesterday.

Focusing on gratitude shifts my mind and heart away from seeing areas of my life as problematic, worrisome, or lacking and toward acknowledging the abundance, what is working *well*. I try to bring this sense of appreciation to all the events in my day. Eating meals, for example. We have a tendency in our busy lives to eat meals while looking at a computer screen or talking on the phone or watching TV or driving. At home or at work, I often leave my laptop at my desk, find a comfortable place to eat, and take time to enjoy my meal. I reflect on all the people it took for the meal to appear in front of me—the farmers who grew the food, the truckers who transported it, and the chefs who prepared it, people I will probably never be able to thank. Then I enjoy the food with a heightened sense of appreciation. Through reflection and appreciation, I try to use daily events to help establish a greater sense of gratitude in my life.

Almost every day, I feel deeply grateful for my spiritual teachers and for the doors they opened in my thinking and my consciousness. We came together completely by luck when I was a teenager and, in my mind, undeserving of their gift to me. Their teachings have changed the way I live, increasing my gratitude for all things, especially for my parents and the life they gave me, the unconditional love they have for me, and all they taught me: to treat everyone with grace and dignity. To operate as a tight-knit family unit that circled the wagons when anyone was in distress. To always remember the humble village roots where their lives had started. And to be grateful for the social mobility we experienced. I could repeat the list of all that my parents gave me every day and still not tire of it.

Of course the one thing I'm most grateful for, which will make most people think, *That's it?*, the one thing I could list each and every day without fail—my cup of masala chai. Cardamom, ginger, cinnamon, fennel (to name just a few of the spices), honey, and warm milk. Amazing. Delicious. It tastes like home. People may criticize me for drinking caffeine, but I don't care. I won't give up my masala chai.

I'm also completely addicted to the daily exercise of gratitude. It's like breathing for me, and for pretty much everyone I've recommended it to. I've always said that gratitude is very powerful and one of the easiest, simplest, and most affordable forms of internal practice, prayer, and meditation. No matter our faith, our beliefs, our circumstances, we can practice giving gratitude. Anyone can point to any of us and challenge us to name ten things we are grateful for, and each and every one of us can be grateful for this one thing—that we have life itself. In the Hindu and Buddhist traditions, they say that if you're born in a human body, you have to be enormously grateful, because in the human body, through the human experience, you find the pathway for the personal evolution of your consciousness. So we can all be grateful for our human bodies and the opportunity we've been given to raise our consciousness. When we don't have that sense of gratitude—and I say this without judgment, because I do mean *we*, because I have been there, and I still go there—when we don't practice gratitude, I believe we lower the quality of our lives and the quality of our being.

As mentioned, Amandine and I still exchange lists of things we're grateful for using online chat. For 15 years, Amandine has worked for the United Nations in 25 countries around the world, most of those countries in conflict or coming out of it. She spent much of those 15 years specifically in Afghanistan. She worked in the most potentially dangerous place she could be—the ballot recount center in Kabul, heavily observed by international representatives and U.S. government officials, the number one target for the Taliban. One night, when she'd finished work and was back at the briefing center, she noticed I was online. There I was, answering e-mail, and suddenly a message popped up: *What are you grateful for?* And off we went, back and forth. Sitting in the midst of war, all that violence, she was calmly going through this gratitude exercise with a friend more than 7,000 miles away, both of us finding a moment of great respite and shifting of mental energy. Through the Internet, Amandine and I were able—in the midst of unrest—to connect with ourselves and with each other.

With our technology today, we can connect with almost anyone to do this exercise. We can talk about what we're grateful for on a cell phone or in text messages. If you have older children, you can check in by texting. You can pick up your phone or text your daughter in college, who's not contacted you for three days, and ask, "What are you grateful for today?" Isn't that a much better way to connect than asking, "Why haven't you called?"

life-intolerant, yet sacred environment revered by the local Native American tribes. But during those seven days, that spot in the desert is one of the most creative, magical, loving communities on the planet. It is astonishing.

Except for that epicenter of commerce—where you can purchase beverages and ice—everyone in the community gives to each other as acts of service. Everything is wildly available, a highly imaginative explosion of offerings. You can go to a free yoga class, stop by the HeeBeeGeeBee Healers camp for a massage, take away a burrito or a boxed curry, or visit Sacred Spaces to attend a workshop on emotional freedom. You can freak dance to Chic at a '70s disco. Immerse yourself in the art—a writhing, 168-foot-long metal and fire interactive serpent created by the Flaming Lotus Girls, or an immense temple of recycled sheets of wood designed by David Best that is burned to the ground near the end of the festival. And, of course, the Man, the Burning Man, a lonely sentinel who watches over the city for seven days before he's burned down in a massive tribal ceremony reminding us that, ultimately, everything is reduced to a pile of dust or ashes, from which someone or something new will rise to repeat the cycle.

Artists share their art, for the sheer beauty of it, for the pure act of expressing themselves, and to bring joy. Others can appreciate their creativity, of course, but you don't pay. You can't pay. It's that simple. Giving doesn't allow for rewards and recognition. It just allows you to give of your creative energy in a selfless way. The art is not only visual. You'll find healing arts, culinary arts, dance, and music. And even me. I perform at Burning Man. This year, I brought The Kirtaniyas, a kirtan music group. I performed with them, singing vocals and playing on my *tanpura*. The experience was earthy, joyous, juicy, and delightful. Anyone can enjoy the experience of sharing your art. You don't need to have talent; you just need to have enthusiasm. Many at Burning Man aren't particularly talented, but nobody cares. The idea is that if you want to perform, you can just get up onstage and sing and dance whatever way you want. Radical inclusivity means everyone is welcome.

There are guidelines in the city, of course, and a set of ten principles reflecting the community's ethos and culture that everyone follows, principles such as Civic Responsibility, Gifting, and Communal Effort. But everyone also assumes an enormous amount of personal responsibility for their own survival and well-being, creating an environment in which creativity flows freely without too many regulations or constraints. One law prohibits cars within the city, allowing bicycles and pedestrians only. Under that same law, the Department of Mutant Vehicles (DMV) allows car *art* in the city—magical tricked-out vehicles driven through the desert at five miles per hour or less for all to see. Night or day, the people who drive these vehicles are extraordinarily cautious, so there are rarely any accidents. What both baffles and fascinates me is how at Burning Man, the self-regulatory system works so amazingly well, even though there are few repercussions for stepping outside the lines. People drive carefully, and there are very few accidents. Yet in our highly penalized system outside Black Rock City, where the repercussions are many and sometimes severe, people ignore them, and we have all sorts of accidents and incidents because of it.

I'm grateful that such an incredible vehicle for expression as Burning Man is available, where everyone brings so much to the table and all from a totally selfless place.

A place where anything is possible. Under the harsh sun beating down on Black Rock City, housing arrangements in ramshackle shelters seem straight out of the Flintstone era. It's as if clothing has just been invented, baffling some, who don't bother with it, and captivating others, who, decked in wild costumes, flood the streets. And everywhere, wheel-based contraptions navigate the city. It's Bedrock all over again with Fred and Wilma spinning through town in their torn-canvas-roofed car, rolling on the newly invented wheel, wild with what's next.

And when the sun sets, there's fire, the desert ablaze with neon, flame-licked art, and lights, thousands of solar- and battery-powered lights. The city's two personalities, prehistoric by day, uber-neotech by night, shifting from one to the other, creating a totally synergetic and enchanting environment.

Two years ago, Larry Page, the CEO of Google, was speaking at the Google I/O developers' conference, and he made the point that the world of technology needs something like Burning Man. He said that in the technology world, we need a place people can go—for a month or a year—where we don't have to worry about restrictions in the mainstream world that would prevent us from building certain kinds of technology. I think that is a reason why so many tech people go to Burning Man, and why the founders of Google have been going all these years, to see the art of what is possible in that wide-open utopian environment and bring it back. A stint in such a community could catapult all types of innovation and creativity—no matter what the field.

I've been going to Burning Man for ten years. Year after year, that weeklong experience is different every time, but always transformational. I keep going back, and I will continue to go back for the rest of my life, for the sheer purpose of being a part of the promise of what human beings are capable of when given the freedom to be exactly who we are. I'm drawn back to Burning Man by the social humanity that shines through the people there and through whatever it is that they do. I'm drawn by the connection, the warmth, the selfless expression, of which each of us is capable.

Somehow with the way we live in the "regular" world, that expression and connection often seem to get lost, but at Burning Man, everyone's innate beauty and humanity shine through, and, as a result, everyone looks beautiful there. It's because they are being authentic. They don't have to be someone else. For once they can shed all their inhibitions and pretenses and just be themselves. They can do what fulfills them. That's another reason to visit the city, to remind ourselves of who we are, and bring that realization back with us. If we're content with our lives, our inner light shines through our eyes. We look beautiful. It's inevitable.

THE DIVINE
ESSENCE OF THE
PORTA-POTTY MAN

It's the last weekend of Burning Man, and I've been standing in the porta-potty line for five minutes. "Sorry for the inconvenience," the sign reads. "We're closed for cleaning." I wait. It's hot. Dry. Gritty. Sand blows everywhere, swirling around the cleaning crew as they haul jugs of blue disinfectant, refill the hand sanitizer from gallon bottles, stock toilet paper with dedication and professionalism.

Fifty-thousand-plus people attend Burning Man, and each of us relies on the porta-potty crew. In that moment, observing the crew in action, I'm overcome with gratitude, and I step out of line to give each of them a big hug. In the spirit of Burning Man, they, like the rest of the "burners," wear colorful costumes. And in the spirit of Burning Man, I give them a handcrafted gift I brought from India and tell them simply, "Thank you for your participation and contribution to this festival. Thank you for making Black Rock City livable and functional."

Meanwhile, the rest of the "burners" are getting restless. "What's that dude talking about?" they want to know.

"He's holding us up." I nod to the burners, step back in line. I'm amazed at the efficiency with which we all handle waste at Burning Man, and I'm in awe of this crew, the dignity with which these people do their jobs, and the position this crew holds in our temporary society. At Burning Man, we're all equal. We all haul out our garbage, leaving the desert in better condition than we found it. Even though the porta-potty crews are here doing a job, rather than attending the festival, they do their job in the same gifting spirit.

The porta-potty crews aren't doing this job because they have no other choice, as in India. It's their business. I'm not saying it's a glamorous job, and I'm not suggesting the crews love their work. But the work differs from what I witnessed growing up in India. Though the basic job is the same, it's been professionalized here. There is some degree of self-respect. Watching the crew finish up, I can't help but compare how vastly different their lives are from those of the people who collected waste when I was growing up in India.

For a while, we lived in Kozhikode in Kerala, a city of two million, where the indoor plumbing and sanitation had not quite reached the entire city. Although our house had plumbing, many had no septic tank or sewage system, just outdoor pit toilets. Members of the scavenger class, the *Thotis,* what is considered the lowest caste, hauled human waste from the outdoor pit toilets away in buckets or carts. These people were born into this work. Their parents collected waste, and so, by birth, they were preordained to collect waste—a job nobody else would touch.

Although they performed a service for all those who were not predestined collectors of waste, the untouchables were not thanked. They were ignored. As a kid, I didn't understand the system or why certain people and not others were saddled with the job of hauling human waste and garbage. All I knew was what I saw from the school bus—waste collectors pushing their carts through the streets—and that these waste collectors were not allowed in my grandmother's house.

While not as prevalent as in the past, the old system of collecting waste is still practiced in many parts of India. With all types of garbage. Even with the new systems, in much of India, garbage collection is inefficient. In my parents' city of Thrissur, they have a waste management system where trucks dump their contents in a designated disposal area. Until two years ago, the trucks dumped garbage in an open residential site with no processing or treatment. The community complained. "Everyone else's garbage is coming into our backyard," people said. "Our kids are falling sick." The residents told the municipality to dump the waste somewhere else other than their neighborhood, but the dumping continued.

Civil disobedience ensued. Women and children in the neighborhood lay down in front of the trucks. When the municipality tried to outsmart the protesters, sending the trucks to dump at night, the women and children stayed up to wait for them, lying in the road to block the trucks. Because they had no place to dump the waste, the trucks stopped picking up garbage in my parents' neighborhood and everywhere else in the city. Eventually, the waste management system for the entire city essentially collapsed. The solution would have been for the two parties to come to an agreement, but they haven't, and two years later, there is no system to remove garbage. Zero. Nothing. People either dump trash in someone else's backyard or they burn it.

Other parts of the world, though certainly not all, have long since solved the problem of dealing with waste. In the case of Thrissur, I feel the failure to solve the problem is due to a lack of imagination and leadership. And it's not just the city my parents live in. I visit many places in India, sacred places where I have a spiritual connection, such as the temple town of Vrindavan, where Krishna was born, and garbage lines the streets. I feel as though I want to step into the midst of that mess, set up a system, and just take care of the problem.

Sometimes I fantasize about setting up a movement in India for garbage collection that would be self-sustaining and generate income from managing waste by composting and recycling. Most important, my movement would train people who are now socially at the bottom of the waste management system to do these jobs. We'd ask clients to sign a contract, obligating them to treat all employees politely, with dignity and respect. If a client were to break the rule once, we'd issue a warning. Twice, another warning. The third time, we'd cancel the contract, and the client would need to be responsible for his or her own household waste.

I picture my calling card reading "Chief Garbage Collector." I see myself showing up for my Wharton reunion and handing out my card to former classmates. I don't imagine, with my profession, that there would be a long line of Wharton MBA students contacting me for career advice, or that I'd be invited to be the graduation speaker. My colleagues who are managing directors at Goldman or McKinsey would beat me to that.

My spiritual teacher Rama Devi said that we should all give the greatest amount of respect to those who come to our house and clean the kitchen and wash our clothes, who haul waste, because we should see them as the divine showing up in human form—they are doing the things that we don't want to do, so that our lives are more comfortable. Rather than treating them badly just because they do what are considered menial jobs, we should treat them with the greatest respect. This was her way of saying that everyone's job is important, and everyone is doing something important, particularly people who are doing those jobs that are seen as undignified. Without these people, our lives would be such a mess. So we should view those who do these jobs as the divine in human form.

Mahatma Gandhi, too, saw these jobs as sacred acts of service. When he instituted social reformation in India, he broke the shackles of the caste system and embraced the lower caste. Instead of referring to the members of this caste as scavengers, Gandhi called them *Harijan*. The word *hari* means God, and *jan* means people—the people of God. Not of a lesser god but of the same god worshipped by higher castes as well.

If you spend time in a traditional ashram, they may ask you to clean the toilets. Everyone does all jobs—decorating the shrine, reading the scripture and giving a sermon, baking the *rotis* in the kitchen, cleaning the cowshed, and taking out the dung—it's all sacred work. "The best way to find yourself," Gandhi said, "is to lose yourself in the service of others." And oddly, no matter what service you're doing, because this service is the commerce of the ashram, you feel your work is sacred because all work is necessary to the whole.

I often think of my time spent in ashrams when I work late at Google and the cleaning crew comes to empty the trash. It would be easy to continue working, to give them their privacy and keep to myself. But I feel a need to turn away from my computer, offer a greeting, share a moment of connection. I've emptied trash. They empty trash. We're all contributing to the Google ecosystem.

At Google, from the highest engineer to those who clean the offices, everyone has a job to do that's critical to the whole. If you think about it, society is no different from a computer with a huge interdependency among parts, a constant exchange of information between security systems and peripherals that breathe input and output. We bow to the screen resolution, the memory, and the central processing unit. But without the humble cooling fan, our computers would burn up.

This interdependency of sacred work and service is why I love the radical inclusivity of Burning Man. It's why I fantasize about creating a waste-management movement—to pay homage to the divine in the most mundane of tasks and situations, to help others realize and appreciate how much we need and rely on each other, that we're all of us, each of us, part of a whole.

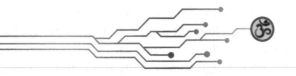

MEETING THE DALAI LAMA

Dharamsala, November 2010.

His Holiness the Dalai Lama is coming toward us to greet us. I am astonished.

We are in his residence, on a verandah surrounding a courtyard where a simple but beautiful garden blooms with Himalayan flowers. The Dalai Lama calls himself just a simple Buddhist monk. And he lives the principle. As we are ushered toward the room where he meets his visitors, he is approaching *us* to receive us and take us in. He walks forward, slightly stooped, eyes curiously taking in the detail, while listening to a lama explaining to him who the visitors are. I am humbled by his gracious gesture of hospitality.

It has all happened very quickly. Though I have had "Meet the Dalai Lama" as a line item on my life list for more than ten years, this opportunity has materialized almost overnight. When it started looking more and more possible—even though nothing would be definite until I actually got there—I made my decision and bought my ticket on a Friday at 5 P.M. in San Francisco, jumped on a plane Saturday morning, and traveled 36 hours through Hong Kong and New Delhi, finally arriving on a small propeller plane Monday afternoon in the tiny Gaggal Airport, with a single flight each day. Within an hour a taxi ride with Lama Phunso, the Dalai Lama's personal tailor, took me up through some clouds and through a mystical Himalayan landscape, depositing me in another world— the tiny settlement of McLeod Ganj outside Dharamsala. Tiny houses clung perilously to the steep hillside, small pathways snaked their way around the Kangra Valley. Monks in russet robes and thick boots walked toward the monastery. Though people increasingly argue it's becoming noisy and choked with traffic, to me, Dharamsala is still a beautiful and tranquil village, perched in the foothills of the Himalayas. For more than 50 years, this has been the home of the Tibetan government in exile, and of Tenzin Gyatso, His Holiness the 14th Dalai Lama of Tibet: the spiritual and temporal leader of the Tibetan people; the winner of a Nobel Prize for peace; a global spokesperson for peace, compassion, and human values; and a beacon of hope for a troubled world.

At 8:30 A.M., when I show up at the Dalai Lama's house and meet Lama Tenzin Dhonden, who is arranging the visit and has just flown in from London, it is the first time I have final confirmation that I will indeed be meeting His Holiness at around 9:30. By then of course the Dalai Lama will have been up for six hours. He wakes up at 3:30 each morning for his meditation and monastic practices even when on the road, meditating for four hours on the roots of compassion.

Already long lines of Tibetans have formed outside the gate to get their customary and traditional audience. Immediately after us there is a group of more than 200 Western visitors—the Old Dharamsala Wallahs, students of the Dalai Lama who lived in Dharamsala in the '60s and

'70s and are back for a reunion visit, this time with their children and grandchildren. I am reminded that the Dalai Lama has a punishing schedule in his multiple roles as head of the Tibetan government in exile; spiritual head of the six million Tibetans around the world; global spokesperson for peace and human ethics; Buddhist scholar and monk; head of the Gelug school of Tibetan Buddhism; and teacher, practitioner, and interpreter of an extremely complex philosophy.

Yet he exudes calmness and alertness. A remarkable presence. He holds me by the hand and asks me if I am Indian. Then he leads us into a simple and modest meeting area and seats us on couches. There are five visitors from the United States that Lama Tenzin has invited to meet with His Holiness. I am struck by how fully present and engaged he is, making eye contact with each person in the room, listening intently to us when we introduce ourselves or ask questions, drinking in the details he sees. He may have complex Buddhist dialectic debates to settle and meetings with world leaders to prepare for. But for now he makes us feel like the most important people in his life.

Years of speaking to audiences around the world have taught the Dalai Lama to come to a level of simplicity that is most appropriate to each audience. I think he understands that simplicity is the ultimate sophistication. Along with simplicity, he also conveys a sense of being very practical. With one sentence he cuts through knots of doctrinal confusion. "You will see contradictory teachings in Buddhism," he tells us. "And the reason is not that the masters were confused. But different teachings are appropriate for people with different dispositions."

He talks about technology and the modern world; he is very interested in how his message is reaching a million people via Twitter, including many in China. "Sometimes you have to take lessons from the devil," he says, and laughs. He explains that he is grateful for India and considers himself a son of India, after his body has been nourished by Indian rice and dal for the last 40 years. "Though the big boss may not like it," he says with a glance at the Buddha's picture, and laughs again. He talks about neuroplasticity, about religious tolerance, about transparency in government. Journalists, he says, should be like elephants. They should sniff officials in the front and then in the back and expose what is really going on.

Most of all, a deep sense of joy pervades his presence. Sometimes even a trace of mischief. It starts with a twinkle in his eye, a wicked smile, a rolling laugh that builds up as a rumble in waves till finally his whole body is shaking. "Ho, ho, ho," he laughs like a Buddhist Santa Claus. I think to myself that he is like manifested joy.

He tells us about a time when he was staying with friends in the United States. While brushing his teeth, he peeked into the medicine cabinet—"illegally," he says with a glimmer of that mischief—and found that they had tranquilizers. Even though they had a level of affluence that most of the people he deals with could not conceive of, they had no peace of mind. They had their freedom, their wealth, but no peace of mind, and they needed tranquilizers to provide it.

"What I saw disturbed me," he says. And we talk about how much of humanity seems to need external chemicals and substances to find peace. The use of antidepressants has surged across the rich world over the past decade, according to the Organisation for Economic Co-operation and Development, raising concerns among doctors that the pills are being overprescribed. Figures show that doctors in some countries are writing prescriptions for more than one in ten adults, with Iceland, Australia, Canada, and the other European Nordic countries leading the way. In China, the antidepressant market has grown by about 20 percent for each of the past three years, albeit from a lower base. Separate data from the United States show that more than 10 percent of American adults use these medications, and that the United States is the largest consumer of antidepressants per capita in the world.

We have the tools to help us find a truer peace in a better way, the Dalai Lama tells the group of us sitting on couches around him. Tools like meditation. But these tools have not yet reached a large segment of the world or people are unaware of these tools. So people use unhealthy tools instead and try to impose peace from the outside. That is not to say many can't benefit from medication when they need medical help. In these cases, medication does not replace meditation, it supports meditation. What His Holiness wants us to understand is that, as power comes from stillness, outer peace can come only from inner peace.

From the moment he stepped forward to greet us, he has been astonishingly gracious with his time and with himself. Posing for pictures, signing pictures, putting *kattas* on everyone, holding our hands like an old uncle meeting his nephews. When it is my turn to say good-bye and thank you, I cry, his humanity has been so great.

Some years ago a few European newspapers ran a poll and asked their readers to pick from a group of leaders the one they respected the most. The readers picked the Dalai Lama over and above other world leaders, including then U.S. President George Bush. I wondered about the fact that here was a person who lacked all the conventional forms of power, wealth, authority, and so on. As a Buddhist monk, he owned nothing, and as a refugee he did not even have a passport of his own. Yet the reason he commands the respect of the world is his moral authority, his commitment to peaceful resolution to geopolitical problems, his incredible sense of compassion and forgiveness, and the simplicity with which he articulates it all free of rhetoric.

His message is simple. World peace, outer peace, and happiness can only come from inner peace. And inner peace has to start with each individual. It starts with a practice of compassion, gratefulness, and respect for others, and of mindfulness in our own lives.

NEXT >

We are at an incredible confluence of events made possible by technology. Yet much of what we are seeing and experiencing now merely hints at what is possible. In 10 to 20 years, the number of human beings on this planet connected to the Internet could climb from three billion to seven billion. And it's not only people that will be connected, but also our homes, our cars, our pets. Within the next few years, these technologies will become incredibly inexpensive—the smartphones that we carry will be in everyone's pocket. With our phones' translation capabilities, there will be no language that cannot be understood by another human being. You will be able to speak in English to a speaker of Russian, and on their end, sound as though you're speaking in Russian in your own voice.

Such enormous possibilities! But to live in this new world opening to us, to adapt to the demands of the world that will emerge, we'll need new rules for living. Our children will need new rules. Going forward, more than ever, we'll need to tune in to our inner technology and bring it into balance with our outer. In many cases, we can draw on the old ways that still serve us, the wisdom traditions where we benefit from 2,500 years of experimentation—trial and error—by other human beings. This is a guidebook that never goes out of date. Yet it is dynamic. We can build on it. Move forward. For in our world, in our lives, even though we can learn from the old ways, we can't click the "Back" button. We have to click "Next."

In the November 2010 issue of *Tricycle* magazine, Reggie Ray, founder of Dharma Ocean Foundation, beautifully captured how to embrace what comes next. "As our practice deepens," he wrote, "we realize that in us there is a love for everything that is; and it doesn't matter how big or how small, how ugly or how beautiful, how blissful or painful it may be; at the very core of the human person is an unconditional and unlimited passion and caring for what is. . . . It's trust in what it means to be human and willingness to let the river of life flow through us, come what may."

Next >

TECH SUPPORT

The answers and help you need are somewhere out there, and the 79th organ in the human body (your smartphone) can take you there. In just one click. Here are some of the destinations I have found useful. But beware of the potential for endless and aimless distraction. Stay focused. Find what you need. Return to your center. Return to your inner-net.

Start Up

- **Google.** Search. A little welcoming box on a sparse white page. One hundred billion times per month humanity stops here and asks their life's greatest questions. And the Google God knows it all. Gateway to collective human knowledge: www.google.com.

- **Lonely Planet.** Before taking off for Dubai, Asunción, or Cincinnati, stop by Lonely Planet to find out everything you need to know about your destination: www.lonelyplanet.com.

- **My website.** Wander through my site, step into my shoes, and see my world. I would be more than happy to see yours. It would be a privilege to have you visit: www.kallayil.com.

THE INTERNET TO THE INNER-NET

- **YouTube.** Find music, how-to, news, entertainment, strange human pursuits, and an infinite trove of videos of every persuasion in all major languages: www.youtube.com.

Purge Your Files

- **The 4-Hour Workweek.** Learn brilliant tips about how to streamline your life so you can focus on what truly matters to you: www.fourhourworkweek.com.

- **GetFriday.** Outsource tasks to a virtual assistant—round the clock: www.getfriday.com.

- **TaskRabbit.** Locate pre-approved contractors in your neighborhood to take on tasks—almost any task—you need help with. I got help with tricking out my Burning Man bike: www.taskrabbit.com.

Recharge and Plug into the Inner-Net

- **Insight Meditation Society.** Study insight (vipassana) and loving kindness (metta) to begin or deepen your meditation practice. Try the ten-day Vipassana retreat. It's 14 hours of meditation every day. Total silence. No reading, writing, or music, not even eye contact. Just you and your thoughts. As I told my friends before leaving for the retreat, I will come back fully enlightened or stark raving mad: www.dharma.org.

- **International Sivananda Yoga Vedanta Centres.** Explore the four main paths of classical yoga in a traditional Indian ashram setting: www.sivananda.org.

Some of my favorite settings are:

- Sivananda Yoga Farm, Grass Valley, California: www.sivanandayogafarm.org

- Sivananda Ashram Yoga Retreat, Bahamas: www.sivanandabahamas.org

- Sivananda Yoga Vendata Dhanwantari Ashram, Neyyar Dam, India: www.sivananda .org.in/neyyardam

- **New Camaldoli Hermitage.** Embark on an inner journey on the craggy Big Sur coast in California with 11 mostly silent Camaldoli monks with a killer URL: www.contemplation.com.

- **Search Inside Yourself Leadership Institute.** Contact SIYLI to bring Chade-Meng Tan's groundbreaking leadership training to your organization. Offers programs for the practitioner and instructor trainees: www.siyli.org.

- **Wisdom 2.0.** Locate international one-day conferences and annual gatherings dedicated to "living with deeper wisdom, compassion, and awareness" in an increasingly fidgety digital world. Founded by Soren Gordhamer. Google "Wisdom 2.0 conference" for current locations.

Connect with All the Other Inner-Nets

- **Amanuddin Foundation.** Help Afghan people deal with the stress of a long, drawn-out war and post-traumatic stress disorder. Founded by Amandine Roche, a force of nature. Based on the wisdom the Dalai Lama espouses—outer peace can only come from inner peace: www.amanuddinfoundation.org.

- **Heifer International.** Empower people to change their lives. Partnering with other donors, you can gift a family with a goat, a pig, a chicken, or even a portion of a larger animal, such as a cow. In turn, the family on the receiving end will pay it forward: www.heifer.org.

- **Kiva.** Through this San Francisco–based organization, any of us can give microloans to women in the Third World starting small businesses. Twenty-five dollars gets you started. You don't need to start a foundation to start having an impact on an international development front: www.kiva.org.

Stretch the Boundaries, Expand the Network

- **Outward Bound.** Stretch physically, mentally, emotionally, and spiritually in Outward Bound's wilderness retreats: www.outwardbound.org.

- **Toastmasters International.** Strengthen your communication on all fronts—from public speaking to telephone conversations to job interviews to date nights. Perhaps most important, even get heard by your spouse: www.toastmasters.org.

- **Tony Robbins.** Operate at your peak performance and live to your highest potential: www.tonyrobbins.com.

Play in the Creative Lab

- **Burning Man.** Sign up for a week of radical self-expression and self-reliance in the middle of the Nevada desert: www.burningman.org.

- **Jason Becker.** Tune in. Talented rock guitarist felled by ALS continues to create music with the last muscles he can still control—his eyes. A source of inspiration for all humans: www.jasonbeckerguitar.com.

- **Touré-Raichel Collective.** Listen to Israeli keyboardist and composer Idan Raichel and Malian singer and guitarist Vieux Farka Touré. They produce incredibly beautiful music: www.toureraichel.com.

Seek Intelligence and Wisdom Beyond the Internet

- **Mata Amritanandamayi, Amma.** Meet Amma, the "hugging saint," with the simple message of love and service, magnificently demonstrated through her humanitarian work and tireless travel and welcoming arms: www.amma.org.

- **Rama Sakti Mission.** Explore the teachings of Rama Devi, whose core message is about "Ghrihasth-ashram," or making your home the primary place for exploring your inner journey. My teacher and the person who taught me meditation and the spiritual path: www.ramasaktimission.org.

- **His Holiness the 14th Dalai Lama of Tibet.** Find endless wisdom on compassion and our interdependency from the Nobel peace laureate, plus publications, talks, international visits, and activities: www.dalailama.com.

ACKNOWLEDGMENTS

An "Attitude of Gratitude" is one of the chapters in my book. And in many places, I acknowledge that it is that mysterious thing called "grace" and the kindness and support of so many people, sometimes complete strangers, that has propelled my life forward. This is where I get to honor and acknowledge many of them.

Most important, my parents, two people from extremely modest backgrounds, who surrounded my siblings and me with love and encouragement. They watched us push past educational and professional boundaries, of which they admittedly had no understanding, letting us do our own thing, with the complete trust that we knew what we were doing, would make the right choices, and would turn out okay. Thank you, Amma and Achan.

My spiritual teachers, Divine Mothers Rama and Tara Devi, who showed me the light, taught me to meditate, and left me signposts that continue to anchor and guide my life. And to Amma, Mata Amritanandamayi, for showing me through her own life that love and service are the best ways to plug into your inner-net.

My first yoga teachers, Swami Vishnudevananda and Swami Sankarananda (Robert Moses), who trained me to become a yoga teacher in an ashram in India when I was a teenager and yoga was not as hip and trendy as it is today.

And Robert, my favorite "Hin-Jew," thank you for expanding my horizons and not getting stuck in the incongruity that an Indian lad was learning a 600-year-old Indian tradition from a white South African Jewish man turned swami in orange.

My siblings, Sathi, Kala, and Ravi, and their families—Manoharan, Sudhakaran, Manju, Shalini, Devi, Jojo, Devyani, and Kalyani—who showed me the power of a tight-knit family, one that rallies around one another and circles the wagons when one of us is in distress.

Patty Gift and Nancy Levin from Hay House, who startled me at Wanderlust Tahoe one year, coming up to me after I'd finished speaking and saying, "When you're ready to write a book, we're ready to publish it." And just like that, I had an offer. Thank you for believing in me.

And leading up to that offer, Leigh Ann Loggins, who accurately predicted that I'd have a book contract within a year. She also encouraged me to hold up Wayne Dyer as my role model. Miraculously, Wayne's publisher, Hay House, approached me first. I didn't want to talk to anyone else.

Stephanie Tade, my agent and publishing mom, who showed up at Google and walked barefoot with me around the campus. The book was behind schedule, and I had no path to finish. So Stephanie, who was driving me to San Francisco that day, used the hour in the car to scold me, and drawing on her years of experience, came up with a miracle solution that manifested this book. Thank you, Stephanie, for your faith in me.

And the miracle and angel was Kelly Malone. I want to build a shrine for her. She figured out that if she told Azha, my personal assistant, to lock me up in the house on Sunday mornings and set me up on my balcony, overlooking the lake, in front of a steaming cup of Rishi masala chai, that in one hour, over three cups, two chapters would tumble out of my brain. She magically transformed my confusing storylines and sometimes pure nonsensical utterances into something intelligible that everyone can enjoy and understand. Plus, she knows the English language. I mean things like apodosis and protasis, disjuncts and antecedents, and to beware of past perfect progressives and dangling modifiers. Thank you, Kelly. This book would simply not have seen the light of day but for you.

Anne Barthel, my tireless editor and woman of infinite patience at Hay House, who could see past my many failings. You did an amazing job of pushing me further and of shaping and deepening this book. Thank you.

Reid Tracy, CEO of Hay House, who invited me to their office in Carlsbad, California, and at the end of the conversation simply said, "We would love to sign you up." Thank you for believing in an untested and unknown author.

Leah Foley, my Irish transcriber, in Dublin, who could listen to my mutterings with an Indian accent coming over the Internet and find meaning, poignancy, and humor. And bloody hell. Despite the whiskey she sipped to keep pace with my masala chai addiction, she could listen well and accurately record what I was talking about.

Amandine Roche, a goddess, supermodel, force of nature, and international woman of mystery. Your work and life inspired me, transformed my life, and found their way into the book. And many of the chapters were graced by your presence, edits, and encouragement.

Malaika, my princess and goddaughter, whom I dote on and love to spoil. There is no softer spot in my heart than the one you occupy.

Azha Broussard, Nisha Raman, Grace Ku, and Silvia Cabrera, the four lovely ladies who manage me—keep my life organized and my schedule sane, book my tickets, and get me to the right place in the right country at the right time on the right plane. And in between, make sure that I have enough time for sleep, yoga, and meditation (and save time for me to write); send flowers to people I love on time; and call my parents on Sunday nights. Thank you for your kindness, generosity, and superior organizational skills, such as getting me organized for Burning Man and trips to Antarctica.

Sukumar Ramanathan, who for the longest time has been one of my closest and dearest friends, and whose prodigious intellect, eclectic knowledge, and awareness of the world have shaped much of my own world. From Mensa membership to running marathons to Burning Man to climbing Kilimanjaro, it was Suku who sparked my discovery. He's recommended almost every single useful book I've read. And he led me to Pico.

Pico Iyer, another prodigious intellect, a man of letters, gifted writer and speaker, and delightful explorer of the world and cultural accidents—thank you for writing my foreword.

Ananta Govinda, my producer and web publisher, thanks to you, my music project became a reality.

Sadhguru Jaggi Vasudev, the mystic who during a lunch meeting at Google discussed how everything we experience in this world has to be processed by our bodies, brains, and minds. His words created a fundamental shift in my thinking, and became the seed idea for my first talk, which led to this book.

Jennifer Barr, who invited me to speak at TEDx Berkeley and while introducing me called my speech "The Internet to the Inner-Net." That speech launched the journey that led to many talks, essays, and this book. Jennifer should take full credit for the title.

Chade-Meng Tan, the Jolly Good Fellow of Google. It was your pioneering spirit and experiments with search (inside yourself) that gave me a platform at Google to bring my own yoga and meditation practice to the company. I am eternally grateful for your contributions to Google.

Jonathan Rosenberg, my mentor at Google, who pointed me toward several great career opportunities. The man who, more than anyone, appreciates my passion for public speaking. My career at Google would not have blossomed the way it has without your mentoring.

Vic Gundotra, another mentor and hero, one of the most charismatic, polished, and persuasive communicators I've seen at Microsoft, at Google, and in the world. You've done wonders for my career and professional growth. And on top of it all, you're an inspiration and a tremendous human being.

Krishnan Nair, Appukutty, and Sukumaran, my teachers at the modest Kendriya Vidyalaya in Koshikode, India, who gave me my love for physics, math, leadership, and public speaking. Look where it's all taken me in my life.

Mejda Das, my kirtan teacher, for delightful moments of playing harmonium and singing in Sanskrit at Google, my home, and many other places.

Meena D'souza and Sriram Ramachandran, Malaika's parents, for all the years I've known them, most of my life, have been the most gracious and caring of friends. I disappear from their lives frequently, and when I reappear, it means I'm in trouble and need help, and their doors and hearts have always been open.

Maureen Bradford, from the first day I met you at Wharton to every day now at Google, you have been a tremendous supporter, angel, and friend.

Stuart Newton, my coach and mentor. At pivotal moments and during life crises he has shone the light. His wisdom, "Happy Human is the highest title," is why my card says what it does. His famous phrase—"When the universe opens a door, you *must* walk through it"—led me to have a personal meeting with the Dalai Lama.

Rania Succar, Suzie Reider, Margo Georgiadis, Alan Eagle, for believing in my talents and giving me the space and freedom to write this book and practice my passion for public speaking through what I do.

Jim Lecinski, my mentor and inspiration for most of my time at Google, a strong supporter of my writing and speaking interests, and an outstanding, nurturing human being.

Alma Sandoval, Luis Sandoval, Kulvi Maisov, Teri Bigio. You created a haven and sanctuary for me to sit on weekends, look at the water, and let the chapters flow.

Manpreet Vohra, shining star in the Indian Foreign Service and fellow adventurer in places as far apart as Hong Kong, Mongolia, Peru, Kenya, Tanzania, and Burning Man, much of which became material for the book. Thanks to you and Naseem for hosting me in these places, and for being among my closest friends in the whole world.

Neha Sangwan, we share an agent, a publisher, speaking platforms, and much respect and love. We promised that we would support each other as writers and speakers, and we are. But you're two steps ahead of me, and I'm learning from you.

Mike Robbins, I could say all the things about you that I say about Neha, but you were a pioneer, already writing and speaking. You were the first person who told me to believe in this dream, while we were sitting in Slice on the Google campus. And I listened to you. Here I am.

Susan Wojcicki, David Pottruck, and Mike Nelson, at some point in my life you said or did something that had a profound impact on me. Thanks for letting me use your stories.

Rikard Steiber, one of my Google managers, who steered me toward my current career and always believed in me.

Henry Miller, my speaking coach—thanks to him I polished my skills and eventually made it to the semi-finals of the world championships of public speaking, and the professional career and success it has led me to.

Chris Lipp, for goading me to become a better public speaker through coaching, mentoring, and competing.

Soren Gordhamer, for creating the Wisdom 2.0 platform that set the stage for many things I write about in this book and speak about. Thank you for ignoring my foolish advice, delivered with great pomp at Yoshka's on the Google campus, and launching Wisdom 2.0 anyway. Thank you, too, for inviting me to speak at so many of the conferences.

Jon Ratcliffe, Dawn and Ivan Suvanjieff, Loren Groves, Ria Tobaccowala, Jeremiah Harmsen, and Don Eisenberg, who were all instrumental in making both the epic Dalai Lama events happen.

Richard Shell, my favorite professor at Wharton and another inspiration for me to want to write. Alka Kapoor, my lovely and gracious host in Hong Kong and Cyprus and a dear lifelong friend. Cari Widmyer and Sarah Bates, Googler friends, for the wisdom you shared that's in this book.

And for a long list of friends who have touched my life in so many ways, many of which are reflected in this book: the NIT gang of Jaap, Mali, Kumar, Mag, Sandy, and Lala; the IIM gang of Shanks, Paddy, Deven, Hash, John, Naren, Shyam, Maya, and Rocks; Professors Mike Useem and Anjani Jain at Wharton; and Wharton classmates David Hinton, Ben Terk, Coop, Laura, TT, and Kelly.

Thank you again. Namaste, and many blessings. This book is a testimony to your love and caring, and to how, collectively, we can birth a completely new idea or product out of thin air.

ABOUT THE AUTHOR

Weinberg Clark Photography in Mountain View

Gopi Kallayil is Chief Evangelist of Brand Marketing at Google. He works with Google's sales teams and customers and helps grow customer brands through digital marketing. In his prior roles he worked as Chief Evangelist for Google+, led the marketing team for the company's flagship advertising product, AdWords, in the Americas and Asia Pacific, and the marketing team for AdSense, Google's publisher-facing product.

Before joining Google, Gopi was on the management team of two Silicon Valley venture-funded start-ups. While a consultant with McKinsey & Company, he worked on engagements helping the management teams of large corporations improve business performance and maximize revenues. He has also led large information technology projects for global corporations in India, China and the United States.

Gopi earned his bachelor's degree in electronics engineering from the National Institute of Technology in India. He received his master's in business administration degrees from the Indian Institute of Management and the Wharton School at the University of Pennsylvania.

Gopi is an avid yoga practitioner, triathlete, public speaker, global traveler and Burning Man devotee. He has spoken at TEDx, Renaissance Weekend, the World Peace Festival, Wisdom 2.0, Yoga Journal LIVE! and Wanderlust. Gopi hosts a TV programme on cable and YouTube called *Change Makers*. He founded a yoga programme at Google for Googlers, called Yoglers. His writings have been published in *The Huffington Post, India Currents, Knowledge@ Wharton* and *Common Ground*.

www.kallayil.com

NOTES

NOTES

NOTES

NOTES

NOTES

NOTES

Hay House Titles of Related Interest

YOU CAN HEAL YOUR LIFE, the movie,
starring Louise Hay & Friends
(available as a 1-DVD programme and an expanded 2-DVD set)
Watch the trailer at: www.LouiseHayMovie.com

THE SHIFT, the movie,
starring Dr Wayne W. Dyer
(available as a 1-DVD programme and an expanded 2-DVD set)
Watch the trailer at: www.DyerMovie.com

▽▲▽

A FIELD GUIDE TO HAPPINESS: What I Learned in Bhutan about Living, Loving and Waking Up, by Linda Leaming

A MINDFUL NATION: How a Simple Practice Can Help Us Reduce Stress, Improve Performance and Recapture the American Spirit, by Congressman Tim Ryan

MIRACLES NOW: 108 Life-Changing Tools for Less Stress, More Flow and Finding Your True Purpose, by Gabrielle Bernstein

All of the above are available at your local bookstore,
or may be ordered by contacting Hay House (see last page).

▽▲▽